Indian Parliament and Democratic Polity – Varied Musings

Indian Parliament and Democratic Polity
– Varied Musings

Ravindra Garimella

BLACK EAGLE BOOKS
Dublin, USA | Bhubaneswar, India

Black Eagle Books
USA address:
7464 Wisdom Lane
Dublin, OH 43016

India address:
E/312, Trident Galaxy, Kalinga Nagar,
Bhubaneswar-751003, Odisha, India

E-mail: info@blackeaglebooks.org
Website: www.blackeaglebooks.org

First International Edition Published by
Black Eagle Books, 2025

**INDIAN PARLIAMENT AND DEMOCRATIC POLITY
– VARIED MUSINGS**
by **Ravindra Garimella**

Copyright © Ravindra Garimella

All rights reserved. No part of this publication may be reproduced, stored in a retrieval system, or transmitted, in any form or by any means, electronic, mechanical, photocopying, recording or otherwise without the prior permission of the publisher.

Cover & Interior Design: Ezy's Publication

ISBN- 978-1-64560-643-7 (Paperback)
Library of Congress Control Number: 2025930955

Printed in the United States of America

CONTENTS

Foreword	07
Preface	09
Tiranga – Tricolour, the Indian National Flag	11
Constitutional Values	21
The Maze around the Mace: Sengol and transfer of Power	36
Indian Parliament House – Journey through time: Tracing the historical evolution of India's Parliamentary structures	43
Procedural Devices available to Members of Parliament	47
Budget – Basic facts & budgetary terminology	78
No-Confidence Motion – A broad overview	85
Status of Members expelled from political parties	93
Understanding White Papers: A brief overview	98
Marriage equality and 17 October, 2023 Supreme Court Verdict – An overview	101
The Enduring value of the Commonwealth: A perspective from the India Region	119

MALLIKARJUN KHARGE
Leader of Opposition
in the Rajya Sabha

43, Parliament House,
New Delhi-110 001
Tel.: 011-2301 6707, 2303 4883
Fax : 2379 3433

Foreword

India's Parliament stands at the heart of our democracy—a forum for rigorous debate, dissent, and the shaping of our nation's future. Over the years, this institution has shouldered the complex responsibility of channelling the aspirations of a diverse people into meaningful laws and policies. In times of both progress and challenge, it has adapted, steadfastly upholding democratic values.

In *Indian Parliament and Democratic Polity – Varied Musings*, Ravindra Garimella brings readers a rich and insightful account of Parliament's foundational role, informed by his four decades as a parliamentary bureaucrat. This collection of essays spans themes ranging from the Tiranga, our constitutional values to, matters related to Anti-defection Law, marriage equality, and more. Each topic reflects the vibrant legacy of our Parliament, weaving historical context with contemporary issues that resonate deeply with India's democratic journey.

The book also explores procedural devices available to MPs, shedding light on the mechanisms that empower representatives and enhance legislative debate. The reflections on the Budget, no-confidence motions, and Commonwealth connections further reveal the intricacies of our parliamentary system and India's engagement with global democracy.

Writing this foreword brings me great satisfaction, as this volume will undoubtedly serve as an essential reference for students, scholars, and all who seek a deeper understanding of India's democratic polity. This compilation offers valuable insights into the traditions and principles that continue to shape our Republic.

(Mallikarjun Kharge)

New Delhi
November, 2024

Residence : 10, Rajaji Marg, New Delhi - 110 011. Phone : 011-2379 3068, 2379 3082
Bengaluru : No. 289, 17th Cross, Sadashivanagar, Bengaluru - 560 080. Tel.: 080-2361 5555, 2361 8888
Kalaburgi : "Lumbini", Alwan-e-Shahi, Area, Kalaburgi - 585 102. Tel.: 08472-255 555

Preface

Indian Parliament and Democratic polity – varied musings is a collection of eleven articles of mine. Based on my observations, instincts and gathered over a period of 4 decades now, as a parliamentary bureaucrat. I have been contributing articles on topical issues pertaining to Indian Parliament and our country's democratic polity. The topics covered in this compilation cover a wide gamut ranging from origin of Indian National Flag, constitutional values, Budget, No-Confidence Motion, Enduring value of Commonwealth *vis-à-vis* India, just to name a few. The intent behind each article is to share with people core of the matter dealt with in the article. These articles were published in different journals at different points. The thrust of this compilation is to bring all these articles in one book for benefit of ready reference by readers.

I am beholden to Shri Mallikarjun Kharge, Leader of Opposition, Rajya Sabha and President of Indian National Congress for kindly writing a foreword to this book.

I express my sincere thanks to Dr. Nandini Sahu, Professor of English, IGNOU for her support and motivating me to bring out this book. My sincere thanks to Shri Divakar Yadav for his tireless constant efforts in assisting me in bringing out the manuscript of the book. My earnest appreciation and thanks to Ms. Abiruchi Shrivastava and

Shri Kush Sharma for providing research inputs for the article on 'Constitutional Values' and 'Marriage Equality – Supreme Court's judgement of 17 October, 2023' respectively.

Last but not the least, my sincere thanks to the team of Black Eagle Books for taking this book to a global readership.

It is my fond hope that compilation of articles in my book are found useful by all those interested in working of Indian Parliament and our country's democratic polity.

Ravindra Garimella

1

Tiranga – Tricolour the Indian National Flag

Its amazing significance

India past 75! These three magical words evoke an immense sense of pride within the hearts of all Indians as we celebrated 78th anniversary of Indian Independence. At this momentous juncture, the Indian national flag stands out as one of the most visible manifestation our democratic polity. In this context it of great interest to note significant milestones vis-à-vis evolution of TIRANGA – TRICOLOUR as the Indian National Flag is popularly and lovingly known. The thrust of this article is to bring to fore the amazing journey of evolution of Indian National Flag (facts gleaned from various sources).

Genesis

As per available sources it was between 1904 and 1906 that first Indian Flag came into existence. It was by an Irish disciple of Swami Vivekananda, Sister Nivedita.

Unofficial Version in 1906

In India the first national flag is said to have been hoisted on 07 August, 1906 in the Parsee Bagan Square (Green Park, Calcutta, source Deccan Herald). The flag was composed of three horizontal strips of red, yellow and green with *Vande Mataram* in the middle. It is believed to have been designed by freedom fighters Sachindra Prasad Bose and Hemchandra Kanungo. The red strip on the flag had sun and a crescent moon and the green strip had eight half open lotuses. The second flag was hoisted in Paris by Madam Bhikaji Cama and her band of exiled revolutionaries in 1907. Being similar to the first flag, the modification being that the top strip had only seven stars denoting the Saptarishi. This flag was also exhibited at a socialist conference in Berlin (source Deccan Herald). Another source indicates that Madam Bhikaji Cama unfurled the first version of Indian national flag—a tricolor of green, saffron and red stripes at the International Socialist Congress held at Stuttgart, Germany in 1907.

As per this very source Lokmanya Bal Gangadhar Tilak and Dr. Annie Besant hoisted the third flag during the Home Rule movement. This flag had five red and four green horizontal strips arranged alternately with seven stars in Saptagiri configuration. One corner of the flag had a star and crescent and on the other corner of the flag was the Union Jack (at the pole end)

Origin of Indian Flag

The origin of the Indian flag in its present format is based on flag designed by Shri Pingali Venkayya, a Andhra youth who presented this to Mahatma Gandhi at All India Congress session at Bezwada (now Vijayawada) in 1921.

Shri Pingali Venkayya was an Indian freedom fighter and a staunch follower of Mahatma Gandhi. This flag consisted of the colours associated with the two principal religions, red for the Hindus and green for Muslims (This flag was based on Swaraj flag). Gandhiji modified the flag by adding a white strip representing the remaining religious communities in India. Hence the tricolor with the spinning wheel on the white background was 'unofficially' adopted at AICC Bezawada Conference in 1921. *This was the origin of 'Tiranga'/Tricolor.*

The flag adopted by Congress at 1921, AICC Session came to be associated with nationhood for India and it was officially recognized at the AICC session held at Karachi in August, 1931.

This was the landmark in the history of the Indian flag

A resolution was adopted that tricolor was India's national flag. At the same time, the current arrangement of stripes and the use of deep saffron instead of red were approved. To avert any communal or sectarian associations or interpretations to the original proposal, new attributes were associated *saffron, white and green stripes*. These were, *saffron* for courage and sacrifice, *white* for peace and truth and *green* for faith and chivalry.

Adoption of Indian National Flag

A watershed moment came on 22 July, 1947 when through a resolution moved by Pandit Jawaharlal Nehru, the National Flag of India was adopted in its present form by the Constituent Assembly. The spinning wheel in the centre of flag was replaced by blue chakra—the dharma chakra. It would be of great interest to note views expressed by Pandit Jawaharlal Nehru while moving the resolution. Relevant extracts from **Constituent Assembly debates** dated **22 July, 1947** are as under:

"Resolved that the national Flag of India shall be horizontal tricolor of deep saffron (kesari), white and dark green in equal proportion. In the centre of the white band, there shall be a wheel in navy blue to represent the charkha. The design of the wheel shall be that of the wheel (chakra) which appears on the abacuse of the Sarnath, Lion Capital of Asoka. The diameter of the wheel shall approximate to the width of the white band. The ratio of the width to the length of the Flag shall ordinarily be 2:3.

** ** ** **

I feel at the present moment for behind this resolution and the flag which I have the honour to present to this House for adoption, lies history, the concentrated history of a short span in a nation's existence. Nevertheless, sometimes in a brief period we pass through the track of centuries. It is not so much the mere act of living that counts but what, one does in this brief life that is ours; it is not so much the mere existence of a nation that counts but what that nation does during the various periods of its existence; and I do venture to claim that in the past quarter of a century or so India has lived and acted in a concentrated way and the emotions which have filled the people of India represent not merely a brief spell of years but something infinitely more. They have gone down into history and tradition and have added themselves on to what vast history and tradition which is our heritage in this country.

So, when I move this resolution, I think of this concentrated history through which all of us have passed during the last quarter of a century. Memories crowd upon me. I remember the ups and downs of the great struggle for freedom of this great nation. I remember and many in this House will remember how we looked up to this flag not only with pride and enthusiasm but with a tingling in our veins; also how; when we were sometimes down and out, then again the sight of this flag gave us courage to go on.

Then, many who are not present here today, many of our comrades who have passed, held on to this flag, some amongst them even unto death and handed it over as they sank, to others to hold it aloft. So, in this simple form of words, there is much more than will be clear on the surface. There is the struggle of the people for freedom with all its ups and downs and trials and disasters and there is, finally today as I move this resolution, a certain triumph about it a measure of triumph in the conclusion of that struggle.

** ** ** **

This resolution defines the flag which I trust you will adopt. In a sense this flag was adopted, not by a formal resolution, but by popular acclaim and usage, adopted much more by the sacrifice that surrounded it in the past few decades. We are in a sense only ratifying that popular adoption. It is a flag which has been variously described.

Some people, having misunderstood its significance, have thought of it in communal terms and believe that some part of it represents this community or that. But I may say that when this flag was devised there was no communal significance attached to it. We thought of a design for a flag which was beautiful, because the symbol of a nation must be beautiful to look at. We thought of a flag which would in its combination and in its separate parts would somehow represent the spirit of the nation, the tradition of the nation, that mixed spirit and tradition which has grown up through thousands of years in India. So, we devised this flag.

** ** ** **

It will be seen that there is a slight variation from the one many of us have used during these part years. The colours are the same, a deep saffron, a white and a dark green.

In the white previously there was the charkha which symbolized the common man in India, which symbolized the masses of the people, which symbolized their industry and which came to us from the message which Mahatma Gandhi delivered. (Cheers)

Now, this particular charkha symbol has been slightly varied in this flag, not taken away at all. Why then has this been varied? Normally speaking, the symbol on one side-of the flag should be exactly the same as on the other side. Otherwise, there is a difficulty which goes against the rules. Now, the charkha, as it appeared previously on this flag, had the wheel on one side and the spindle on the other if you see the other side of the flag, the spindle comes the other way and the wheel comes this way; if it does not do so, it is not proportionate, because the wheel must be towards the pole, not towards the end of the Flag. 'There was this practical difficulty.

Therefore, after considerable thought, we were of course convinced that this great symbol which had enthused people should continue but that it should continue in a slightly different form, that the wheel should be there, not the rest of the charkha, that is the spindle and the string which created this confusion, that the essential mitt of the charkha should be there, not the rest of the charkha, that is the spindle and the string which created this confusion, that the essential (motif) of the Charkha should be there, that is the wheel. So, the old tradition continues in regard to the charkha and the wheel. But what type of wheel should we have? Our minds went back to many wheels but notably one famous wheel, which had appeared in many places and which all of us have seen, the one at the top of the capital of the Asoka column and in many other places. That wheel is a symbol of India's ancient culture, it is a symbol of the many things that India had stood for through the ages. So, we thought that this chakra emblem should be there, and that wheel appears.

For my part, I am exceedingly happy that in this sense indirectly we have associated with this flag of our not only *this emblem but in a sense the name of Asoka, one of the most magnificent names not only in India's history but in world history. I have mentioned the name of Asoka I should like you to think that the Asokan period in Indian history was essentially an international period of Indian history. It was not a narrowly national period. It was a period when India's ambassadors went abroad to far countries and went abroad not in the way of an empire and imperialism but as ambassadors of peace and culture and goodwill. (Cheers.) Therefore, this flag that I have the honour to present to you is not I hope and trust, a flag of empire, a flag of imperialism—a flag of domination over anybody, but a flag of freedom not only for ourselves but a symbol of freedom to all people who may see it. (Cheers) And wherever it may go—and I hope it will go far, not only where Indians dwell as our ambassadors and ministers but across the far seas where it may be carried by Indian ships, wherever it may go it will bring a message, I hope, of freedom to those people, a message of comradeship, a message that India wants to be friends with every country of the world and India wants to help any people who seek freedom. (Hear, hear)*

That I hope will be the message of this flag ...

** ** ** **

It is stated in this resolution that the ratio of the width to the length of the flag shall ordinarily be 2:3. Now you will notice the world 'ordinarily'. There is no absolute standard about the ratio because the same flag on a particular occasion may have a certain ratio that might be more suitable or on any other. Occasion in another place the ratio might differ slightly. So there is no compulsion about this ratio.

But generally speaking, the ratio of 2:3 is a proper ratio. Sometimes the ratio 2:1 may be suitable for a flag flying on a building. Whatever the ratio may be the point is not so much the relative length and breadth, but the essential design. So, Sir, now I would present to you not only the resolution but the flag itself.

There are two of these National Flags before you. One is on silk-the one I am holding and the other on the side is of cotton Khadi.

I beg to move this resolution. (Cheers)

** ** ** **

Mr. President: I have now notice of three amendments to this resolution.

Mr. President: I would ask Members to express their assent to the Resolution which has been placed before them and show their respect to the flag by getting up and standing in their places for half a minute.

The motion was adopted, the whole Assembly standing.

Thereafter Pandit Jawahar Lal Nehru proposed, *"Sir, may I respectfully suggest that the two flags which have been displayed this morning may be specially preserved and subsequently deposited in the National Museum (Applause).*

Mr. President: I accept that suggestion.

An Honourable Member: I request you on behalf of the House to convey our homage to Mahatma Gandhi and tell him that we are observing the day very magnificently.

Mr. President: I will do that with the greatest pleasure.

Indian National Flag (Its basic attributes)

- The Indian flag is a horizontal tricolor in equal proportions of deep saffron (orange) on the top, white in the middle and dark green at the bottom. Each colour represents something different. *Saffron* stands for courage and sacrifice. *White* represents peace and unity and truth. *Green* stands for faith and fertility.
- **Ashok Chakra has significant place on the national flag.** The Chakra was modeled after the 'wheel of

- dharma' a religious motif from Hinduism, Jainism and especially Buddhism. Ashok Chakra is also called the wheel of duty.
- The most visible use of the Ashok Chakra is at the centre of the Flag of India where it is rendered in a navy blue colour on white background replacing the symbol of Chakra (spinning wheel) of pre-independence version of the flag. The blue colour represents knowledge and cleanliness.
- There are 24 strokes of Dharma Chakra which are the representation of the 24 *Rishis* of the Himalayas in which *Vishvamitra* is first and *Yajnavalkya* the last (source: www.mha.gov.in)
- The Ashoka Chakra is also known as '*Samay Chakra*' in which 24 strokes represent 24 hours of the day and is symbol of movement of time. (source: www.mha.gov.in)
- It is worthwhile to note that Truth or Satya, dharma or virtue ought to be controlling principle of those who work under the flag.

Flag Code of India

A set of laws, practices and conventions that apply to the display of the national flag of India was introduced on 26 January, 2022. Flag Code of India has been divided into three parts. Part1 of the Code contains general description of the National Flag. Part II contains provisions regarding hoisting/display/use of national flag by members of public, private organization, educational institutions etc. Part III comprises of provisions regarding hoisting/display of the National Flag by the Central and State Governments and their organizations and agencies. (source: www.mha.gov.in/Flag code of India)

There has been an amendment to Flag Code of India vide order dated 30.02.2021(at para 1.2 of Part I of the Flag code, 2002) to the effect that "The National Flag shall be made of hand spun and hand woven or machine made, Cotton/polyster/ wool/silk/khadi bunting".

The code has been further amended at para 2.2 of part II to the effect that "(xi)" where the Flag is displayed in open or displayed on the house of a member of public, it may be flown day and night.

Prevention of Insults to National Honour Act, 1971

The Prevention of Insults to National Honour Act, 1971 enacted on 23 December, 1971 is an Act of the Parliament of India which prohibits the desecration of or insult to the country's national symbols, including the national flag, national emblem, national anthem, the Constitution, and map of India including contempt of Indian Constitution. [www.mha.gov.in • Documents • National Flag, Emblem & Anthem]

The Indian National Flag – TIRANGA/TRICOLOUR represents the hopes and aspirations of the people of India.

••

2

Constitutional Values

Constitution of India is bedrock of India's Democratic Polity.

The Constitution of India is one of the most progressive Constitutions world over and was adopted on 26 November, 1949 and the members of the Constituent Assembly appended their signatures to it on 24 January, 1950. In all, 284 members actually signed the Constitution. The Constituent Assembly held in all Eleven Sessions lasting for 165 days. Beginning from 9 December, 1946, the members of the Constituent Assembly held intensive deliberations in the Constitution Hall of Parliament House (now known as Central Hall, Samvidhan Sadan) spanning over a period of two years, eleven months and seventeen days.

On 26 January, 1950, the Constitution of India came into force. This historic day has ever since been celebrated as Republic Day.

26 November, 1949, the day on which the Indian Constitution was adopted by the Constituent Assembly also assumes critical importance and is being observed as

Constitution Day. 26 November, 2024, would mark the 75th anniversary of adoption of Constitution of India.

The values enshrined in the Constitution of India are an outcome of collective wisdom of members of the Constituent Assembly and their views based on Indian ethos of an humanitarian, equitable society and individual dignity.

Every Indian which includes particularly the Indian youth wholly needs to be aware of and comprehend the constitutional values and uphold these.

Values enshrined in Constitution of India

The Constitution of any country serves several purposes. It lays down certain ideals that form the basis of the kind of society that we aspire to live in. A country is usually made up of different communities of people who share certain beliefs, but may not necessarily agree on all issues. A Constitution helps serve as a set of principles, rules and procedures on which there is a consensus.

These form the basis according to which the people want the country to be governed and the society to move on. The Indian Constitution has certain core values that constitute its spirit and are expressed in various articles and provisions.

The vision of the Indian Constitution is clearly reflected in its Preamble.

At the threshold it would be apt to know the historical background in regard to the Preamble.

The Preamble is based on the *Objective Resolution*.

On 13 December, 1946, Pandit Jawaharlal Nehru moved in the Constituent Assembly the Resolution regarding Aims and Objects (Objective Resolution) which laid down the basic principles and objectives that would guide the Constitution making process.

After due deliberation this Objective Resolution was adopted by the Constituent Assembly **on January 22, 1947.**

    Text of the Resolution is:-
    "I beg to move:
1. This Constituent Assembly declares its firm and solemn resolve to proclaim India as an Independent Sovereign Republic and to draw up for her future governance a Constitution;
2. WHEREIN the territories that now comprise British India, the territories that now form the Indian States, and such other parts of India as are outside British India and the States as well as such other territories as are willing to be constituted into the Independent Sovereign India, shall be a Union of them all; and
3. WHEREIN the said territories, whether with their present boundaries or with such others as may be determined by the Constituent Assembly and thereafter according to the Law of the Constitution, shall possess and retain the status of autonomous Units, together with residuary powers, and exercise all powers and functions of government and administration, save and except such powers and functions as are vested in or assigned to the Union, or as are inherent or implied in the Union or resulting therefrom; and
4. WHEREIN all power and authority of the Sovereign Independent India, its constituent parts and organs of government, are derived from the people; and
5. WHEREIN shall be guaranteed and secured to all the

people of India justice, social, economic and political; equality of status, of opportunity, and before the law; freedom of thought, expression, belief, faith worship, vocation, association and action, subject to law and public morality; and

6. WHEREIN adequate safeguards shall be provided for minorities, backward and tribal areas, and depressed and other backward classes; and

7. WHEREBY shall be maintained the integrity of the territory of the Republic and its sovereign rights on land, sea, and air according to Justice and the law of civilised nations, and

8. this ancient land attains its rightful and honoured place in the world and make its full and willing contribution to the promotion of world peace and the welfare of mankind.

Preamble which is the 'soul' of 'Constitution of India' reflects the values enshrined in Constitution of India.

What exactly do we mean by the term 'value'. Instinctively one may say truth, non-violence, peace, kindness, respect, integrity. From a common man's perspective value is *'that which is worth having and observing for the existence of human society as an entity'*.

The Indian Constitution contains all such values, the values that are the universal, human and democratic. The values expressed in the **PREAMBLE** are expressed as objectives of the Constitution. These are: sovereignty, socialism, secularism, democracy, republican character of Indian State, justice, equity, liberty, equality, fraternity, human dignity and the unity and integrity of the nation.

Now a quick look at PREAMBLE.

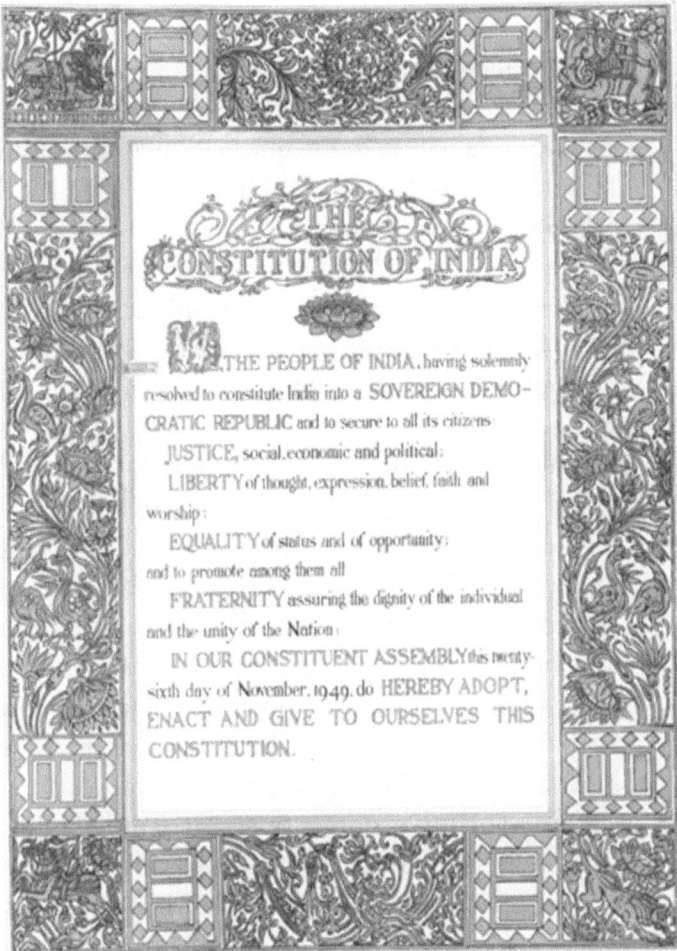

A quick refresher of the Constitutional Values

1. **Sovereignty:** The Preamble declares India "a sovereign socialist secular democratic republic". Being sovereign means having complete political freedom and being the supreme authority.
   - It implies that India is internally all powerful and externally free. It is free to determine for itself without

any external interference (either by any country or individual) and nobody is there within to challenge its authority.
- This feature of sovereignty gives us the dignity of existence as a nation in the international community. Though the Constitution does not specify where the sovereign authority lies but a mention of **'We the People of India'** in the Preamble clearly indicates that sovereignty rests with the people of India. This means that the constitutional authorities and organs of government derive their power only from the people.
2. **Socialism:** The word socialist was not there in the Preamble of the Constitution in its original form. In 1976, the 42nd Amendment to the Constitution incorporated 'Socialist' and 'Secular', in the Preamble.
- The word 'Socialism' had been used in the context of economic planning. It signifies major role in the economy. It also means commitment to attain ideals like removal of inequalities, provision of minimum basic necessities to all, equal pay for equal work.
3. **Secularism:** In the context of secularism in India, it is said that 'India is neither religious, nor irreligious nor anti-religious.' It implies that in India there will be no 'State' religion – the 'State' will not support any particular religion out of public funds. This has two implications, a) every individual is free to believe in, and practice, any religion she/he belongs to, and, b) State will not discriminate against any individual or group on the basis of religion. (Article 15)
4. **Democratic Republic:** The Preamble reflects democracy as a value. As a form of government, it derives its authority from the will of the people. The

people elect the rulers of the country and the elected representatives remain accountable to the people.
- Democracy contributes to stability, continuous progress in the society and it secures peaceful political change.
- It allows dissent and encourages tolerance. And more importantly, it is based on the principles of rule of law, inalienable rights of citizens, independence of judiciary, free and fair elections and freedom of the press.
- The Preamble also declares India as a Republic. It means that the head of the State is elected and she/he is not a hereditary ruler as in case of the British Monarch. This value strengthens and substantiates democracy where every citizen of India is equally eligible to be elected as the Head of the State. Political equality is the chief message of this provision.

5. **Justice:** Justice promises to give people what they are entitled to in terms of basic rights to food, clothing, housing, participation in the decision making and living with dignity as human beings. The Preamble covers all these dimensions of justice – social, economic and political. "Social justice" has been defined in a variety of ways.
- Social justice means equal rights for all, regardless of gender, race, class, ethnicity, citizenship, religion, age or sexual orientation.
- It implies equal rights for women and girls in workplaces, homes and public life. It implies economic justice – which means governments must take active steps to alleviate poverty and redress past injustices. Economic justice really forms a part of social justice. It seeks the equitable distribution of

natural and intellectual wealth so that everyone is able to gain a fair share.

6. **Equity:** Equity derives its spirit from the concept of social justice. It represents a belief that there are some things which people should have, that there are basic needs that should be fulfilled, that burdens and rewards should not be spread too divergently across the community, and that policy should be directed with impartiality, fairness and justice towards these ends.

- It is generally agreed that equity implies a need for fairness (not necessarily equality) in the distribution of gains and losses, and the entitlement of everyone to an acceptable quality and standard of living.
- The Universal Declaration of Human Rights, 1948 states that the 'recognition of the inherent dignity and of the equal and inalienable rights of all members of the human family is the foundation of freedom, justice and peace in the world'.
- Social equity refers to a set of standards which apply to our personal and social relationships with other individuals and/or groups. These standards consist of a bundle of rights and duties which apply to members of certain "deprived or disadvantaged sections" in society.
- The term also covers the protection of certain fundamental rights which we all enjoy as citizens of a free society.

7. **Equality:** Equality is considered to be the essence of modern democratic ideology. The Constitution makers placed the ideals of equality in a place of pride in the Preamble. All kinds of inequality based on the concept of rulers and the ruled or on the basis of caste

and gender, were to be eliminated. All citizens of India should be treated equally and extended equal protection of law without any discrimination based on caste, creed, birth, religion, sex etc.

8. **Liberty:** The Preamble prescribes liberty of thought, expression, belief, faith and worship as one of the core values. These have to be assured to every member of all the communities. It has been done so, because the ideals of democracy cannot be attained without the presence of certain minimal rights which are essential for a free and civilized existence of individuals.

9. **Fraternity:** There is also a commitment made in the Preamble to promote the value of fraternity that stands for the spirit of common brotherhood among all the people of India.

- In the absence of fraternity, a plural society like India stands divided. Therefore, to give meaning to all the ideals like justice, liberty and equality, the Preamble lays great emphasis on fraternity.
- In fact, fraternity can be realized not only by abolishing untouchability amongst different sects of the community, but also by abolishing all communal or sectarian or even local discriminatory feelings which stand in the way of unity of India.

10. **Dignity of the Individual:** Promotion of fraternity is essential to realize the dignity of the individual. It is essential to secure the dignity of every individual without which democracy cannot function. It ensures equal participation of every individual in all the processes of democratic governance.

11. **Unity and Integrity of the Nation:** Fraternity also promotes one of the critical values, i.e. unity and integrity of the nation. To maintain the independence

of the country intact, the unity and integrity of the nation is very essential. Therefore, the stress has been given on fostering unity amongst all the inhabitants of the country.

Our Constitution expects from all the citizens of India to uphold and protect the unity and integrity of India as a matter of duty.

12. **International Peace and a just International Order:** The value of international peace and a just international order, though not included in the Preamble is reflected in other provisions of the Constitution.

    The Indian Constitution directs (Directive Principles of State Policy Part IV) the state (a) to promote international peace and security, (b) maintain just and honourable relations between nations, (c) foster respect for international law and treaty obligations, and (d) encourage settlement of international disputes. To uphold and observe these values is in the interest of India. The peace and just international order will definitely contribute to the development of India. (Article 51)

13. **Fundamental Duties (Article 51A):** Our Constitution prescribes some duties to be performed by the citizens. It is true that these duties are not enforceable in the court of law like the fundamental rights are, but these duties are to be performed by citizens.

Fundamental duties have great importance because these reflect certain basic values like patriotism, nationalism, humanism, environmentalism, harmonious living, gender equality, scientific temper and inquiry, and individual and collective excellence.

Fundamental Principles and Beliefs

- Constitutional values also refer to the fundamen-

tal principles and beliefs that underpin a country's constitution, which serves as the supreme law of the land.
- These values provide the foundation for the legal and political framework of a nation, guiding its governance and ensuring the protection of the rights and liberties of its citizens. Some of the basic constitutional values are:-
  ➢ **Rule of Law:** This principle ensures that all individuals and institutions, including the government, are subject to and accountable under the law. It implies that no one is above the law, and everyone should be treated equally and fairly.
  ➢ **Democracy:** Many constitutions uphold the value of democracy, emphasizing the importance of government by the people, for the people. Democratic values often include free and fair elections, the protection of minority rights, and the separation of powers among different branches of government.
  ➢ **Equality:** Constitutional values often promote equality before the law and equal protection of the law, ensuring that all citizens are entitled to the same legal rights and opportunities, regardless of their race, gender, religion, or other characteristics.
  ➢ **Individual Rights:** Constitutional values typically enshrine individual rights and liberties, such as freedom of speech, freedom of religion, the right to privacy, and the right to a fair trial. These rights protect individuals from government overreach and guarantee their freedoms.
  ➢ **Human Dignity:** Many constitutions emphasize the inherent worth and dignity of every human being. This value underlies the protection of individual

rights and the prohibition of inhumane and degrading treatment.
- **Justice:** Constitutional values often include principles of justice, which encompass fairness, equity, and the impartial administration of the law. Access to justice and the right to a fair trial are essential components of this value.
- **Secularism:** Some constitutions promote the separation of religion and the state, ensuring that the government remains neutral regarding religious matters and protecting the freedom of religion for individuals.
- **Sovereignty:** Constitutional values often reflect the concept of national sovereignty, which asserts the independence and self-determination of a nation. This can include protection against external interference and respect for a nation's territorial integrity.
- **Social Welfare and Justice:** Some constitutions include provisions for social justice and welfare, emphasizing the government's role in ensuring the well-being of its citizens and addressing economic inequalities.
-

These constitutional values are the fulcrum on which the nation's legal and political system rest and seeks to serve as a guide for the actions and decisions of government officials and institutions. They are often protected through legal mechanisms, such as constitutional rights and judicial review, to ensure their enforcement and protection.

Pledge by members of Constituent Assembly

The commitment of Members of Constituent Assembly for upholding constitutional values is reflective from the pledge which they had taken in the special midnight session.

The fifth session of the Constituent Assembly of India commenced in the Constitution Hall (Central Hall of Parliament House, now renamed as Samvidhan Sadan), New Delhi, at 11 pm on August 14, 1947. In the special midnight session, Jawaharlal Nehru passed a motion requesting the members to take a pledge as the clock strikes midnight. The full resolution as read out by Pandit Nehru before the Constituent Assembly is popularly known as the "Tryst With Destiny' speech. As the clock struck twelve, all the members took the following pledge:-

"At this solemn moment when the people of India, through suffering and sacrifice, have secured freedom, I.......... a member of the Constituent Assembly of India, do dedicate myself in all humility to the service of India and her people to the end that this ancient land attain her rightful and honoured place in the world and make her full and willing contribution to the promotion of world peace and the welfare mankind."

It would not be out of place to mention here that constitutional values can vary significantly from one country to another, reflecting the unique history, culture, and political context of each nation. A snapshot view of constitutional values in different countries I have appended as an Annexure.

Critical importance of Constitutional Values

The critical importance of constitutional values more so in the present day scenario cannot be overstated.

It is incumbent upon each one of us as a citizen of this country to uphold constitutional values.

ANNEXURE

Snapshot view of constitutional values in different countries

1. United States:

Individual Rights: The U.S. Constitution's Bill of Rights protects fundamental individual rights, including freedom of speech, freedom of religion, the right to bear arms, and protection against self-incrimination.

Democracy: The U.S. Constitution establishes a democratic system with regular elections, separation of powers, and a commitment to government by the people.

2. Germany:

Human Dignity: The German Basic Law (Grundgesetz) places a strong emphasis on human dignity as a foundational value.

Federalism: Germany is a federal republic, and its constitution grants significant powers to individual states (Länder).

3. South Africa:

Equality: The South African Constitution promotes equality and prohibits discrimination based on various characteristics, including race, gender, and sexual orientation.

Social Justice: The Constitution emphasizes the pursuit of social justice and the protection of economic and social rights.

4. Canada:

Bilingualism and Multiculturalism: The Canadian Constitution recognizes English and French as official languages and promotes multiculturalism to respect cultural diversity.

Indigenous Rights: Canada's Constitution acknowledges the rights and interests of Indigenous peoples.

5. **Japan:**
Pacifism: The Japanese Constitution, following World War II, includes a commitment to pacifism, renouncing the use of military force to settle international disputes.
Rule of Law: The Constitution upholds the rule of law and guarantees the protection of individual rights.

6. **Norway:**
Social Welfare: The Norwegian Constitution includes provisions related to social welfare, ensuring citizens' access to education, healthcare, and social services.
Monarchy: Norway's Constitution establishes a constitutional monarchy with a hereditary monarch and a parliamentary system of government.

7. **Israel:**
Jewish Identity: The Basic Laws of Israel recognize the country as a Jewish and democratic state, reflecting its identity as both a homeland for the Jewish people and a democracy for all its citizens.
Protection of Religious Freedom: Israel's Basic Laws protect the freedom of religion and conscience for all residents.

These examples illustrate the diversity of constitutional values around the world. Each country's constitution reflects its history, culture, and unique challenges, and the values enshrined in these documents play a crucial role in shaping the legal and political landscape of the respective nations.

****

3

The Maze around the Mace : Sengol and transfer of Power

On 23 May, 2023, Prime Minister of India placed **'Sengol'** in Lok Sabha Chamber in New Parliament Building on the right hand side of the Speaker's Chair. The sittings of both Houses of Parliament in New Parliament Building (which has now been notified as Parliament House of India) from 19 September, 2023. What exactly is 'Sengol'?

'Sengol' is a spectre. It would be of interest to note the historical background and its relevance. *Sengol* can be traced back to historical spectre from Tamil Nadu in possession of pontiffs of Thiruvavaduthurai Adheenam mutt. There had a claim that Sengol was handed over to Pandit Jawaharlal Nehru, India's First Prime Minister, by pontiffs of Thiruvavaduthurai Adheenam mutt on the eve of India's independence, which marked transfer of power between the British and India. There appeared a further claim that on this occasion Pandit Nehru consulted Shri C. Rajagopalachari, the last Governor General of India and on his suggestion Pandit Nehru received the Sengol. As reported on a social media post, the mutt itself claimed that both Lord Mountbatten and Pandit Nehru had reached out to the Thiruvavaduthurai Adheenam to enable this transfer of power.

These claims, however, are not supported as such by any historical records.

History of Spectres

Spectres had been/have been used widely across the world.

In UK Houses of Parliament, two ceremonial *maces* represent the monarch's authority. The monarch is referred to as the "third part of Parliament" and signs Bills into law. Parliament cannot lawfully sit, debate, or pass any legislation without a royal *mace* being present in the chambers. They are carried into and out of the two chambers in procession at the beginning and end of each day.

On the rare occasion that a monarch addresses both houses in Westminster Hall, for example in 2012 for Elizabeth II's Diamond Jubilee, the Lords and Commons *maces* both are present, and are covered with a red and a green cloth respectively when he or she enters the hall.

The House of Lords has two *maces*, one of which is carried by the Usher of the Black Rod and placed behind the Lord Speaker on the Woolsack before the House sits. All members are required to bow their heads to the *mace* upon entering the chamber. It is absent when the monarch delivers his or her speech from the throne at State Openings of Parliament. The other *mace* accompanies the Lord Chancellor on official duties outside the House of Lords. *Mace A* made in the reign of Charles II, 1672, is 1.56 m (5.1 ft) long and weighs 11.21 kg (24.7 lb). *Mace B* made in the reign of William III and Mary II in 1695, is 1.58 m (5.2 ft) long and weighs 11.82 kg (26.1 lb).

The House of Commons *mace*, carried by the Serjeant-at-Arms, is placed on brackets on top of the Table of the House in front of the Speaker. When the Commons sits as a Committee of the Whole House, or when Finance Bills are discussed, the *Mace* sits under the table. It is 1.48 m (4.9 ft) long and weighs 7.96 kg (17.5 lb).

Position in India

When India got independence, certain customs and traditions of Westminster were adopted, some were adapted to be in consonance with the Indian ethos. For instance, the practice of placing 'Mace' in both Houses of Parliament; wearing of wigs and robes by Presiding Officers and Clerks of Houses and officers at the Table were not adopted. Instead the Secretaries-General and officers at the Table wear buttoned up tunics in keeping with the Indian tradition.

Spectres – a Chola tradition

Spectres were a part of the Chola tradition, as also been part of Tamil culture for centuries before the Cholas. The Tamil epic Thirukkural, dated between 3rd century BCE and 5th century CE, dedicates a chapter each to the 'Right Spectre' and the 'Cruel Spectre'. But the spectre as a mark of sovereign power is neither unique to Tamils, or Indians. In so far as origins of spectre it dates back as per available sources, to 8th century BCE, where a reference to spectre was made in a plaque of Tiglath-Pileser III at Ashur (also spelled as Assur) the modern Qal at Sharqat, ancient religious capital of Assyria, located on the west bank of the west bank of the Tigris river in northern Iraq.

Sengol vis-à-vis transfer of power

There is no authoritative historical record referring symbolic transfer of power using a spectre.

Yasmin Cordery Khan in her book 'The Great Partition', mentions that a number of religious rituals were part of the celebrations. In the book, it had been mentioned that the handover of the spectre took place at a private residence as part of the celebration and not as an official ceremony.

In his book "Betrayal in India" DF Karaka gives an account of different events. One being, where Karaka mentions that Pandit Nehru yielded to religious ceremonies as the Independence edged closer and consented to have the blessings of religious pandits. Karaka *inter alia* states *"Even Pandit Nehru, who had never been known to fre- quent the temples or to indulge in much religious ceremony, consented to have the blessings of the religious pandits. From Tanjore there came emissaries of the head priest of the Sanyasis, an order of Hindu ascetics. It was traditional in ancient India to derive power and authority from the holy men. Pandit Nehru yielded to all this religious ceremony because it was said of old of the kings of India that this was the traditional way of assuming power. The mood of New Delhi had become almost superstitious.*

In the evening the priests walked ahead of these religious processions. They carried the sceptre, the holy water which they had brought with them from Tanjore, and rice. They laid their gifts at the feet of the Prime Minister. Holy ash was marked on the Pandit's forehead and the priests gave him their blessings.

Later, at the house of the President of the Constituent Assembly, Dr. Rajendra Prasad, who was also President of the Congress, Pandit Nehru sat round a holy fire; around it the women of the house were chanting hymns. The oldest woman among them made an auspicious tilli mark on the forehead of all the ministers and constitution- makers.

All then left for the Constituent Assembly hall which was gaily decorated in saffron, white and green, for the occasion."

DF Karaka does not make reference of any symbolic transfer of power through handing over a spectre.

Neither do, Mountbatten's last personal report as the Viceroy of India, sent on 16 August 1947; the chapter on 'The Mountbatten Viceroyalty Princes, Partition and Independence' from the book Constitutional Relations between Britain and India: The Transfer of Power 1942-7; The Transfer of Power in India by VP Menon; and even India Remembered: A Personal Account of the Mountbattens during the Transfer of Power by Pamela Mountbatten.

Even in newspaper articles of August, 1947, there has been no mention of Shri Rajagopalachari and Lord Mountbatten seeking for it or of Lord Mountbatten receiving and handing back the spectre to the Adheenam.

Nevertheless as per documented sources, closer to Indian independence Pandit Nehru met and honoured several representatives, which also includes receiving a Sengol from the Thiruvavaduthurai Adheenam. But none of this formed part of any official process of transfer of power.

Transfer of power

The official and formal transfer of power to India was a result of the Indian Independence Act 1947 of the Parliament of the United Kingdom, which received the Royal Assent on July 18, 1947. The Act stated that "as from the fifteenth day of August, nineteen hundred and forty-seven, two independent dominions shall be set up in India, to be known respectively as India and Pakistan." **It is this**

Act and the Royal Assent that marked the transfer of power. There was no requirement for any formal action on the end of Viceroy on August 15, 1947. Even the Act was eventually repealed on January 26, 1950 by the Article 395 of the Indian Constitution.

The fifth session of the Constituent Assembly of India commenced in the Constitution Hall (Central Hall of Parliament House, now renamed as Samvidhan Sadan), New Delhi, at 11 pm on August 14, 1947. In the special midnight session, Jawaharlal Nehru passed a motion requesting the members to take a pledge as the clock strikes midnight. The full resolution as read out by Pandit Nehru before the Constituent Assembly is popularly known as the *'Tryst With Destiny'* speech. As the clock struck twelve, all the members took the following pledge:-

"At this solemn moment when the people of India, through suffering and sacrifice, have secured freedom, I.......... a member of the Constituent Assembly of India, do dedicate myself in all humility to the service of India and her people to the end that this ancient land attain her rightful and honoured place in the world and make her full and willing contribution to the promotion of world peace and the welfare of mankind."

Hence, the power transferred automatically at midnight as per the Indian Independence Act, and the Constituent Assembly assumed power for the governance of India with the pledge mentioned above. The Constituent Assembly then appointed Lord Mountbatten as the Governor General of India from August 15, 1947. With this, the midnight Session came to an end.

The swearing in ceremony commenced at 8.30 am on August 15, 1947, wherein Chief Justice of the Federal Court of India, Sir Hiralal J. Kania, Swore-in Lord Mountbatten as the Governor General. Mountbatten then issued the oath to the new cabinet including the Prime Minister, Jawaharlal Nehru. This ceremonial appointment of the new cabinet by the Governor-General, now by President of India continues till date.

Through this article an attempt has been made to collate information from all available sources with a view to throw light on the relatively lesser known historical background of 'Sengol'. All the sources have been accredited. It is hoped that readers will find the article interesting.

••

Sources:
1. "Betrayal in India" by D. F. Karaka, London, Victor Gollanz Ltd., 1950 pp 38-39
2. The article titled "Sengol and transfer of power to Nehru…." By Santosh Saravanan, published in News minute datelined 26 May, 2023.
3. Regarding UK Houses of Parliament — "Ceremonial Maces in UK;
4. Thorne
5. The Great Partition by Yasim Cordery Khan]

4

Indian Parliament House – Journey through time: Tracing the historical evolution of India's Parliamentary structures

The new Parliament House was inaugurated 28 May 2023. The actual sittings on of Lok Sabha and Rajya Sabha were held *w.e.f.* 19 September, 2023.

It would of interest to have look into its historical perspective starting from 1921, till date. The thrust of this article is to take the readers on a sojourn into the past , starting from origins of existing Parliament House and basic relevant facts of subsequent buildings in Parliament estate.

Speaking of Parliament the Constitution of India in article 79 provides in unequivocal terms that Parliament comprises of President of India, Council of States (Rajya Sabha); and House of People (Lok Sabha). President is an integral part of Parliament.

Old Parliament House

The old Parliament House has now been renamed as 'Samvidhan Sadan'. The Foundation Stone of Parliament House was laid on 12 February 1921 by H.R.H. the Duke of Connaught. The construction of the building took six years and the opening ceremony was performed on 18 January 1927 by the then Governor-General of India, Lord Irwin. The cost of construction was Rs. 83 lakhs.

Parliament House Annexe

With the expansion of Parliament Secretariat comprising of Lok Sabha and Rajya Secretariats the need was felt for a new building for various wings of both the Secretariats other than legislative division, Reporting and Interpretation services. The foundation stone of Parliament House Annexe was laid on the 3 August 1970 by Shri V.V. Giri, the then President of India. It was inaugurated on 24 October 1975 by Shrimati Indira Gandhi, the then Prime Minister of India.

Parliament Library Building (PLB)

Parliament Library, one of the richest repositories of books in India, was established in the year 1921 to assist members of the Indian Legislature.

A library was first set up in Baker's Parliament House in 1921, well before India's independence.

Till May 2002, the Parliament Library was functioning from the Parliament House. With time, the Library service expanded providing multi farious services namely Library & Reference, Research, Documentation & Information Service). The accommodation available to the Parliament Library and its allied services in the Parliament House building over a period of time became too limited to cope with the volume of literature being acquired by it. Besides, there had been a growing demand for making available to the Members of Parliament a more effective, efficient and modern Research, Reference and Information Service. In order to satisfy these requirements, the new Parliament Library Building (Sansadiya Gyanpeeth) was conceived. The foundation stone was laid by Shri Rajiv Gandhi, the then Prime Minister of India, on 15 August 1987 and the Bhoomi Poojan was performed by Shri Shivraj V. Patil, the then Speaker, Lok Sabha on 17 April 1994.

The building has a total covered area of 60,460 sq.m. and has been constructed at a cost of Rs. 200 crore. The construction was completed over a period of 7 years and 9 months. The Parliament Library Building was inaugurated on 7 May 2002 by Shri K.R. Narayanan, the then President of India.

Extension to Parliament House Annexe Building

As parliamentary activities proliferated, further expansion was required, leading to the conception of the Extension to the Parliament House Annexe Building. The foundation stone for this extension was laid on 5 May 2009 by Vice-President Dr. Mohammad Hamid Ansari and Lok Sabha Speaker Somnath Chatterjee. The Prime Minister inaugurated the completed extension on 31 July 2017.

Conclusion

The Parliament House stands unique and significant in the grand scheme of things. The building is positioned higher than other structures within the Parliament Estate, symbolizing its importance. As the core of the nation's political architecture, it houses both parliamentary bodies, reflecting the spirit of democratic governance that forms the cornerstone of the Indian polity.

ANNEXURE
Features of New Parliament House

The new Parliament House, now officially known as 'Parliament House of India', has been broadly stated to be conceptualized keeping in view following parameters.

The triangular architectural building spans 65,000 sq.mt. and seeks to achieve a seamless synthesis of modernity and India's rich cultural tapesty.

Legislative decor

The Lok Sabha Chamber is adorned with a resplendent Peacock-inspired design, and the Rajya Sabha Chamber exudes an aura of Lotus-themed elegance. The Chambers have amplified capacities—988 seats in Lok Sabha and 392 in Rajya Sabha. The Lok Sabha Chamber has eight blocks and Rajya Sabha Chamber has six blocks.

Cutting-edge Workspaces

Workspaces are equiped with avant-garde communication technology, ensuring an uninterrupted services in legislative ambiance.

AV Prowess

Commodious committee rooms are equipped with audio-visual systems, with a view to elevate functionality and efficiency in parliamentary discourse.

Inclusive Haven

A space has been designed to be 'Divyang Friendly', ensuring unimpeded movement for individuals with disabilities.

Central Serenity

There is a central lounge, with a majestic banyan tree, fostering member interaction amidst the lively parliamentary environment.

●●

5

Procedural Devices Available to Members of Parliament

Elected representatives of the people in a democratic polity personify the collective voice, will and thought and the aspirations of the people whom she or he represents in Parliament or a Legislature. Members as representatives of the people bring up matters of public interest concerning the people on the floor of the House.

For achieving this objective, Indian Parliament has been on the forefront. Parliament of India is not only a forum for enacting laws. Legislating is one of its functions. The critical importance of Indian Parliament is that it provides a very effective debating forum. The same is applicable to State Legislatures.

In modern times, Parliaments all over the world have been assuming added responsibilities in response to the growing hopes and aspirations of the people. They are devoting more and more time in the deliberation of issues pertaining to redressal of grievances of the people.

A number of parliamentary devices are available to the members, under the Rules of Procedure and Conduct of

Business of Houses of Parliament and State Legislatures as well as by conventions, to enable them to raise issues, elicit information and obtain decisions of the Government on a variety of matters affecting the public.

These devices afford ample opportunities to the members not only to review the working of the executive but also to constructively criticize the policies, programmes and actions of the Government. These devices are also very useful to the members in *ventilating* public grievances.

Here it would be worthwhile to mention that leaders and senior leaders get enough opportunities to speak on floor of the House as decided by their party leader or Chief Whip. This advantage is not as such enjoyed by other members that is backbenchers, the reason being, any discussion or legislative measure has to be disposed of within the time allocated by Business Advisory Committee or as allocated by the House. That being so backbenchers too have many topical issues affecting their constituents, to raise on the floor of the House and seek adequate redressal.

The thrust of this script is to dwell upon briefly various parliamentary devices available to members in general as also those which benefit backbenchers. In Indian Parliament, no Members are officially referred to in Parliament terminology as 'backbenchers'. This expression is, however, used in an informal manner.

Parliamentary devices available to members of UK Parliament have also been briefly mentioned.

Parliamentary devices in Lok Sabha and Rajya Sabha Rules

Apart from questions, several parliamentary devices are available in Rules of Procedure and Conduct of Business in Lok Sabha and Rules of Procedure and Conduct of Business in Council of States (Rajya Sabha) (as well as State Legislatures) to members for raising urgent matters of public importance requiring immediate attention of the Government. From Rules point of view parliamentary devices can as well be termed as *procedural devices*.

If these procedural devices available under the Rules of Procedures of both Houses of Parliament are able to be put to use gainfully, only then the Members of Parliament would really be able to perform their parliamentary duties and meet their obligations, which they owe to their constituents.

Different procedural devices have different timelines for tabling notices to raise matters.

Each procedural device has its importance. Under which Rule a particular matter can most optimally be raised, in other words, which procedural device can be taken recourse to would depend upon the urgency, criticality and the nature of the matter sought to be raised.

By and large the procedural devices available to members under the Rules of Procedure of both Houses of Parliament are similar, with a few exceptions.

Moving a No-confidence Motion against the Government and raising an adjournment, motion or a censure motion is feasible only in Lok Sabha.

Even in Lok Sabha Motion of No-confidence as such is not relevant in the context of raising matters of urgent public interest by members on a day-to-day basis in the House.

Each of the procedural device has been dwelt upon in simple terms bringing out their significance. The members choose through which parliamentary device they wish to raise a matter. The parliamentary devices range from the more popularly known parliamentary questions to the ultimate device of last resort which is Motion of No Confidence in the Council of Ministers.

Parliamentary devices – general introduction

- As already mentioned a number of parliamentary devices are available to the members, under the Rules of Procedure and Conduct of Business, as well as by convention, to enable them to raise issues to elicit information and obtain decisions of the Government on a variety of matters affecting the public.
- These devices afford ample opportunities to the members not only to review the working of the executive but also to constructively criticize the policies, programmes and actions of the Government. These devices are also very useful to the members in ventilating public grievances.
- Apart from Questions, several parliamentary devices are available to the members for raising urgent matters of public importance requiring immediate attention of the Government. These include Discussion on Motion of Thanks on the President's Address, Adjournment Motion, No-Day-Yet-Named Motion, Short Duration Discussion, Calling Attention, Resolutions, etc.
- Members also have the opportunity to raise matters under Rule 377 of the Rules of Procedure of Lok Sabha and by way of special mentions during 'Zero Hour'. Besides these devices, members also do get opportunities to raise their constituency matters when they participate in the discussion on Railway and General Budgets, which have a very wide scope.
- *For a Member to raise urgent importance on a day to day basis the parliamentary devices like matters under Rule 377/ Special Mentions , Calling Attention and matters under Zero Hour provide optimal utility.*

PARLIAMENTARY QUESTIONS

Types of Questions
Starred Question
[Rule 36 of Lok Sabha Rules and Rule 42 of Rajya Sabha Rules]
- A Starred Question is one to which a member desires an oral answer in the House and which is distinguished by an asterisk mark. When a question is answered orally, supplementary questions can be asked thereon. Only 20 questions can be listed for oral answer on a day.
- Only one such question from a member is allowed
- In Lok Sabha under the provisions of Rule 32 of Lok Sabha Rules "unless the Speaker otherwise directs **the first hour (11.00 hrs to 12.00 hrs)** are available for asking and answering questions.
- In Rajya Sabha under provisions of Rule 38 of Rajya Sabha Rules "Unless the Chairman otherwise directs the **Question Hour shall be from 12 noon to 1 PM.**"

Unstarred Question
[Rule 39 of Lok Sabha Rules and Rule 45 of Rajya Sabha Rules]
An Unstarred Question is one which is not called for oral answer in the House and on which no supplementary questions can consequently be asked. To such a question, a written answer is deemed to have been laid on the Table after the Question Hour by the Minister to whom it is addressed. It is printed in the official report of the sitting of the House for which it is put down. Only 230 questions can be listed for written answer on a day.

Not more than five Unstarred Questions per member are allowed. In a day 1 Starred and 4 Unstarred Questions per member per day are allowed.

Short Notice Question

[Rule 54 of Lok Sabha Rules and Rule 58 of Rajya Sabha Rules]

A Short Notice Question is one which relates to a matter of urgent public importance and can be asked with shorter notice than the period of notice prescribed for an ordinary question. Like a starred question, it is answered orally followed by supplementary questions.

Short Notice Questions are taken up immediately after Question Hour is over.

Separate ballots are held for Starred and Unstarred Questions and results of ballots are displayed on Notice Board.

Assurances

Assurances given by Ministers in replies to questions (or in any other debate) have utmost significance.

While replying to questions in the House, Ministers at times give assurances or undertakings either to consider a matter or to take action or to furnish the further information to the House later.

Such assurances, promises, undertakings etc., given by the Minister from time to time are scrutinized by a Committee on Government Assurances and reported to Lok Sabha on the extent to which such assurances etc., have been implemented and to see whether such implementation has taken place within the minimum time necessary for the purpose *i.e.* 3 months.

Half an Hour Discussions

[Rule 55 of Lok Sabha Rules and Rule 60 of Rajya Sabha Rules]

Members have a right to get information by means of question to Ministers.

Members can utilise this parliamentary device when they feel that the answer given to a question — Starred or Unstarred or Short Notice — is not complete or does not give the desired information or needs elucidation on a matter of fact. On notices being given under Rule 55 of the Rules of Procedure, they may be allowed by Speaker to raise a discussion in the House for half an hour. The procedure is, therefore, termed as 'Half-an- Hour Discussion'.

Half-an-Hours are generally held on three sittings in a week, namely, Monday, Wednesday and Friday. Notices have to be given at least three days in advance and accompanied by an explanatory note.

The discussion is normally limited to half-an-hour and is held in the last half-an-hour of a sitting.

Parliamentary Questions – Impact

Parliamentary Question is indeed a very effective parliamentary device available to members to elicit information from the Government and also ensure executive accountability to the Legislature.

Other important parliamentary devices

Motion of Thanks on the President's Address

Article 87(1) of the Constitution provides for President's Address to members of both the House of Parliament assembled together at the commencement of the first Session after each General Election to the Lok Sabha and at the commencement of the first Session of each year.

Under the provisions of Article 79 of the Constitution, Parliament compromises of **President of India**, Council of States and House of People. As an integral part of Parliament, address to both Houses of Parliament is one of the august functions of the President of India. (This akin to address by crown in UK Parliament)

Discussion on matters referred to in the President's Address takes place on a Motion of Thanks moved by a member and seconded by another member. According to the established practice, the mover and the seconder of the Motion of Thanks are selected by the Prime Minister. The form of the motion is:-

"That the members of Lok Sabha assembled in this Session are deeply grateful to the President for the Address which she/he has been pleased to deliver to both Houses Parliament assembled together on......"

The discussion on Motion of Thanks usually lasts for 3 to 4 days. The scope of discussion of President's Address is very wide and members are free to speak on national or international problems.

Members cannot, however, refer to matters which are not the direct responsibility of the Government of India.

During the discussion, a large number of amendments are moved by the members highlighting certain issues which the President's Address failed to take note of or criticizing the policy enunciated in the Address or making suggestions for Government action.

This is akin to the Address by the Crown in UK Parliament.

Discussion of Union Budget

Till 2017 there used to be two separate Budgets –

Railway Budget which preceded General Budget on 28th or last working day of February of an year. However, from 2017 separate budget for Railways was done away with and was subsumed in General Budget now known as Union Budget.

Discussion on Railway and General Budgets also provides members ample opportunity to raise matters of national importance as well as those concerning their constituencies.

During General Discussion on the Union Budget, members may express their views on the policy of taxation as it is expressed in the Budget; they may also comment upon whether the amount of expenditure ought to be increased or decreased having regard to the importance of a particular item. The general discussion on Union Budget is followed by discussion on Demands for Grants of respective Ministries in second stage of discussion of Budget.

During discussion on Demands for Grants, it is open to members to disapprove a policy pursued by the Government or to suggest measures of economy in the administration or to focus attention of the Government to specific local grievances.

Members can also raise their grievances by moving cut motions to Demands for Grants. All the admitted cut motions are forwarded to the concerned Ministry.

The Ministry concerned takes note of these cut motions and the Minister, while replying to the discussion in the House, may respond to the subject-matter of important cut motions.

Even though the cut motions are ultimately defeated in the House, the Government gets seized of the matter.

Adjournment Motions

[Rule 56 of Lok Sabha Rules]

[This parliamentary device is not available for Members of Rajya Sabha]

- The primary object of a adjournment motion is to draw the attention of the House to a recent matter of urgent public importance having serious consequences and in regard to which a motion or a resolution with proper notice will be too late.
- The adjournment motion is thus an extraordinary procedure which, if admitted, leads to setting aside the normal business of the House for discussing a definite matter of urgent public importance.
- The subject-matter of the motion must have a direct or indirect relation to the conduct or default on the part of the Union Government and must precisely pin- point the failure of the Government of India in the performance of its duties in accordance with the provisions of the Constitution and law.
- Where the Speaker is satisfied *prima facie* that the matter proposed to be discussed is in order under the Rules, she/he may give her/his consent to the moving of the motion, and at the appropriate time, that is, after Question House, call upon the member concerned to ask for leave of the House to move the adjournment motion.
- If objection to leave being granted is taken, the Speaker will ask those members who are in favour of leave being granted to rise in their places and if not less than fifty members rise accordingly, she/he will declare that leave is granted. If less than fifty members rise, the Speaker will inform the member and she/he has not the leave of the House.

- If leave of the House is granted, the motion 'that the House do now adjourn' shall be taken up at 1600 hours or at an earlier hour if the Speaker, after considering the state of business in the House, so directs.
- Where the Speaker is satisfied *prima facie* that the notice of an adjournment motion is inadmissible, she/he will refuse her/his consent without bringing the matter before the House and the member concerned will be verbally informed of the Speaker's decision.
- When the motion is being discussed, that is, from the hour the discussion on an adjournment motion has commenced to the time the motion is disposed of, the Speaker has not power to adjourn the House for the day because during that time the power vests in the House to take a decision on its adjournment.
- Once the discussion commences, it has to be concluded and decision arrived at without interrupting the debate.
- However, there is no bar to taking up formal items *viz.* Laying of papers or having a lunch break during the discussion.
- An adjournment motion involves an element of censure against the Government. In the event of an adjournment motion being adopted, the House automatically stands adjourned.

Although no direct effect can be given to an adjournment motion but it is very likely that a Government which has failed to prevent an adverse vote on adjournment motion, will not be able to survive a direct motion of no-confidence in the Council of Ministers. There has not been any occasion in Lok Sabha of an adjournment motion being adopted. All adjournments admitted and discussed so far had been negatived.

Notices under Rule 267 of Rajya Sabha Rules

It is important to note that since there is no provision for adjournment motion in Rajya Sabha, a notice under Rule 267 in form of motion can be resorted to raise an urgent matter on a particular day.

Informally this can be said to be adjournment motion like device in Rajya Sabha.

This notice under Rule 267 is given in form of a motion. However, admissibility of Motion under Rule 267 solely vests with Chairman, Rajya Sabha.

- Any member may with the consent of the Chairman move a motion under Rule 267 that any rule may be suspended in its application to a motion related to the business listed for the day.
- **Timeline**: Notice can be given upto 6 pm the previous day and latest by 10 am on the day it is proposed to be moved.

No-day-yet-named Motions

[Rule 184 of Lok Sabha Rules and Rule 167 of Rajya Sabha Rules]

The term 'motion' in its wide sense means any proposal submitted to the House for eliciting its decision. Every matter is determined in the House by means of a question put from the Chair on a motion made by a member and resolved either in the affirmative or negative.

Motions are in fact the basis of all parliamentary proceedings. Any matter of public importance can be the subject matter of a motion.

Unless otherwise provided in the Constitution or the Rules, no discussion on a matter of general public interest can take place except on a motion made with the consent of the Speaker (Rule 184).

Procedure when a motion is admitted

On being called by the Speaker, Lok Sabha/Chairman, Rajya Sabha, the first member in whose name the motion stands in the List of Business formally moves the motion and makes her/his speech.

Thereafter, the Speaker/Chairman places the motion before the House.

Amendments or substitute motion, if any, are then moved and discussion follows.

After the members and Minister concerned have participated in the debate, the mover of the motion may exercise her/his right of reply.

If a motion is adopted by the House, it is transmitted to the Minister concerned for appropriate action.

Motions of Confidence and no-confidence in the Council of Ministers

[Rule 198 of Lok Sabha Rules pertains to No Confidence Motion, there is no specific Rule governing confidence motion but it is governed]

[In Rajya Sabha, there is no provision for motion of Confidence Motion]

The motion of confidence and no-confidence in the Council of Ministers cannot, strictly speaking, be termed as parliamentary devices available to members for raising matter in the House.

Once these are admitted, the discussion is not confined to any specific subject.

NO CONFIDENCE MOTION

One of the fundamental postulates of parliamentary democracy is the principle of collective responsibility of the Council of Ministers headed by the Prime Minister to

Lok Sabha – the House of People. This responsibility is joint and indivisible. Collective Ministerial responsibility of the House of People (Lok Sabha) is the crux of parliamentary democracy in India. Article 75(3) of the Constitution of India provides that "The Council of Ministers shall be collectively responsible to the House of People". The Council of Ministers must enjoy the confidence of the House of People to stay in power. Whenever there emerges a situation, when it is perceived that the Government (Party in power) does not enjoy majority support, the well established procedural device of motion of no-confidence under Rule 198(1) of the Rules of Procedure and Conduct of Business in Lok Sabha, is taken recourse to, to test the majority of the Government of the day. Hence, a No Confidence Motion can be raised only in the Lok Sabha. Moving of a No-Confidence could be termed as device (weapon) of last resort when section of Members/Members of Lok Sabha move against the Government, which is indicative of lack of trust in the Government, the ruling dispensation.

In this context, it would be worthwhile to take note of text Article 75(3) of the Constitution which provides that "The Council of Ministers shall be collectively responsible to the House of People".

The text of No Confidence Motion reads as follows :

"That this House expresses it's want of Confidence in the Council of Ministers."

In interpreting Article 75(3), the Supreme Court of India in U.N.R. Rao vs. Smt. Indira Gandhi (A.I.R. 1971, SC) observed:-

"Article 75(3) brings into existence what is usually called 'Responsible Government'. In other words the Council of Ministers must enjoy the confidence of the House of the People. While the House of the People is not dissolved under art. 85(2)(b), art 73(3) has full operation. But when it is dissolved, the Council of Ministers cannot naturally enjoy the confidence of the House of the People... Art. 75(3) only applies when the House of the People does not stand dissolved."

The provisions for moving a No-Confidence Motion are provided for in Rule 198 of the Rules of Procedure and Conduct of Business in Lok Sabha.

The procedure for moving a No-Confidence Motion is explained briefly as under:-

A motion expressing want of confidence in the Council of Ministers may be made subject to the following restrictions:-

(a) leave to make the motion shall be asked for by the Member when called by the Speaker;

(b) the Member asking for leave shall by 10.00 hours on that day give to the Secretary-General a written notice of the motion which such member proposes to move.

As per proviso to this Rule, notices received after 10.00 hrs on a day shall be deemed to have been received at 10.00 hrs on the next day on which the House sits.

If the Speaker is of the opinion that the motion is in order, the Speaker shall read the motion to the House and shall request those members who are in favour of leave being granted to rise in their places, and if not less than fifty members rise accordingly, the Speaker shall declare that leave is granted and that the motion will be taken up on such day, not being more than ten days from the date on which the leave is asked for as the Speaker may appoint. If less than fifty members rise, the Speaker shall inform that the member has not the leave of the House.

If leave is granted, the Speaker may, after considering the state of business in the House, allot a day or days or part of a day for the discussion of the motion.

Thereafter, the Speaker shall, at the appointed hour on the allotted day or the last of the allotted days, as the case may be, forthwith put every question necessary to determine the decision of the House on the motion.

The Speaker, if thinks fit, may prescribe a time limit for speeches.

A No-Confidence Motion is distinct from censure motion. A motion of No-Confidence need not set out any ground or charges on which it is based. The grounds do not form part of the motion. The standard format of No-Confidence Motion is "That this House expresses its confidence in the Council of Ministers".

Once a motion of No-Confidence Motion is adopted, the Government of the day has to resign as it clearly indicates that the Government does not enjoy the confidence/the requisite majority to govern.

Confidence Motion
- There is no specific rule to the motions in the Council of Ministers in the Rules of Procedure and Conduct of Business in Lok Sabha. However, on some earlier occasions as a result of hung Parliaments occasioning the advent of minority governments/formation of co-alition governments, the necessity of the device of the Confidence Motion arose.
- In the absence of any specific rules, the motions of confidence have been admitted under the category of motions stipulated under Rule 184 of the Rules, which are meant for raising discussions on matters of public interest. Decisions on such motions are taken

under Rule 191 of Rules by putting before the House all the necessary questions. The one line notice of motion under Rule 184 reads that "this House expresses its confidence in the Council of Minister." In the case of a confidence motion, there is no requirement for seeking the leave of the House as in the case of no confidence motion. The Confidence Motion gets priority over the no confidence motion even if the notices are received for both motions, basically because under Rule 25, Government business has precedence over other business on days allotted for transaction of government business (Practice and Procedure of Parliament by Kaul &Shakdher (7^{th}Edn., p. 778).

- As the need for Confidence Motion is felt when the legitimacy of the Government is in question, it is in fitness of things that a positive vote confidence is sought for.

As regards Confidence Motions, the following factors are worth noting:-

(i) Need for Confidence Motion arises only in cases of hung Parliament and the legitimacy of coalition Government claiming to form Government is in question.

(ii) Confidence Motion flows from Article 75 of the Constitution. Any motion not covered by Rules is shown as motion under Rule 184 in records.

(iii) There have been twelve occasions so far when the need for Confidence Motions arose and in all these occasions, either there was hung Parliament and/or coalition Governments were formed. To test the majority of Governments so formed, Confidence

Motions were brought forward by the Government (Ruling coalition) mostly on the directions of the President of India.

Briefly the break-up of these Confidence Motions is as under:

(i) 6 LS - 01
(ii) 9 LS - 03
(iii) 10 LS - 01
(iv) 11 LS - 04
(v) 12 LS - 02, and
(vi) 14 LS - 01
(iv) In all these occasions one line motion under Rule 184 reading *"this House expresses its confidence in the Council of Ministers"*, were given and the motion sufficed the purpose.

Short Duration Discussion

[Rule 193 of Lok Sabha Rules and Rule 176 of Rajya Sabha Rules]

This is one of popular parliamentary devices under the Rules. A member desirous of raising discussion on a matter of urgent public importance may give notice under Rule 193 (176 as the case may be). The notice has to be accompanied by an explanatory note stating reasons for raising discussion on the matter in question. Further, the notice has to be supported by the signatures of at least two other members.

As per Rule 194(2), the Speaker may allot two sittings in a week for discussions under Rule 193 and allow such time for discussion not exceeding two hours at or before the end of the sitting, as the Speaker may consider appropriate. (Corresponding provisions are there in Rajya Sabha Rules

176 to 177, while there is no specific provision to the effect, the Chairman may allot two sittings in a week).

Discussion under Rule 193/176 does not involve a formal motion before the House. Hence, no voting can take place after discussion on matters under this rule.

The member who raises the discussion has no right of reply. At the end of the discussion, the Minister concerned gives a brief reply.

Resolutions

[Rules 170 to 183 of Lok Sabha Rules and Rules 154 to 166 of Rajya Sabha Rules]

- A member or a Minister may, subject to the Rules of Procedure, move a resolution relating to a matter of general public interest.
- Resolutions may be broadly: divided into three categories *viz.* (i) resolutions which are mere expressions of opinion by the House; (ii) resolutions which have a statutory effect; and (iii) resolutions which the House passes in the matter of control over its own proceedings.
- Resolutions may also be categorized as: (i) Government resolutions; (ii) Private Members' resolutions; and (iii) Statutory resolutions.
- A resolution must purport to convey the opinion of the House as a whole and not of any section thereof.
- The last two and a half hours of a sitting on every alternate Friday of a session is usually allotted for the discussion of Private Members' Resolutions.
- Government resolutions are subject to the same rules as the Private Members' Resolutions.

Calling Attention

[Rule 197 of Lok Sabha Rules and Rule 180 of Rajya Sabha Rules]

- *The concept of calling attention, which is an innovation in modern parliamentary procedure, is of Indian Origin.*
- A member may, with the prior permission of the Speaker, call the attention of a Minister to any matter of urgent public importance. The Minister concerned thereafter makes a statement.
- A Calling Attention is listed in the names of not more than five members.
- After the statement by Minister, each member in whose name the item is listed, may with the permission of the Speaker ask a clarificatory question, and the Minister replies to all such questions at the end.

This parliamentary device is very effective as in just 40 minutes or so a topical issue is able to be raised in the House with a response from the concerned Minister.

Mistake or Inaccuracy in Statement by Minister or Members

Direction 115 (Directions by the Speaker)

Under this direction procedure has been laid down for pointing out mistake or inaccuracy in statements made by Ministers or Members.

A member may, with the prior permission of the Speaker, Lok Sabha, focus the attention of the House to any mistake or inaccuracy in a statement made by a Minister or any other Member on the floor of the House, if the matter so challenged has an intimate relation to a statement given by a member, or arises out of a question asked by the member.

When a Minister notices that an incorrect information has been given to the House by her/him in answer to starred/unstarred/short notice question or a supplementary question and seeks permission to make or lay a statement *suo motu* clarifying/correcting her/his earlier statement under Direction 16 (by the Speaker), the notice received from member under Direction 115 pointing out the same inaccuracy is not admissible. Further, if the Minister herself/himself wishes to correct a mistake or inaccuracy in the information given by her/him during a debate and seeks to make/lay a statement *suo motu* under Direction 114A correcting such mistake/inaccuracy, the notice received from a member under Direction 115 pointing out such mistake/inaccuracy is also inadmissible. (Sources: provisions under Direction 16, 114A and 115 of the Directions by the Speaker).

By and large, the procedure in Rajya Sabha is similar (Direction 6 of Directions by the Chairman, Rajya Sabha).

Matters under Rule 377 in Lok Sabha

- Matters, which are not points of order can be raised by way of Special Mentions under Rule 377.
- This procedural device provides opportunity to the members to raise matters of general public interest.
- **Timeline:** Notices for matters under Rule 377 given on Friday (or last working day of week if Friday happens to be a holiday) between 10:00 hours to 10:30 hours are valid from Monday to Friday of next week.
- **Outcome:** On each matter raised under Rule 377 by a member a written reply is sent by the Minister herself/himself.

Special Mention under Rule 180A in Rajya Sabha-
- This is akin to matters under Rule 377 in Lok Sabha.
- Matter of public importance can be raised as Special Mention.
- Not more than 2 notices can be given by a member per sitting. These are taken up after laying of papers.
- **Timeline**: Notices upto 5 pm on previous day are valid for the sitting on which sought to be raised [Rule 180C(1)]. Notices remain alive for the week in which these are given.
- **Outcome**: Response of the Government has to be given to the MP within one month of matter being raised.

'Zero Hour'
- This is a unique procedural innovation.
- The emergence of 'Zero Hour', can also be traced to the early sixties when many issues of urgent public importance began to be raised by members immediately after Question Hour, sometimes with the prior permission of the Chair and sometimes without such permission.
- A practice started developing that as soon as the Chair declared that the Question Hour was over, members would be on their-feet to raise matters which were considered or felt to be of utmost importance to be brought to the attention of the House without delay.
- In the 15th Lok Sabha, the procedure for raising of matters of urgent public importance during 'Zero

Hour' has been further revised, *inter alia*, with a view to streamlining the regulation of matters raised therein.
- This practice was further streamlined by the Speaker during the 16th Lok Sabha. As per the present practice, members now can give the notices for 'Zero Hour' after 10 AM on previous day till 9 AM on the day on which members desire to raise their matters in the House.
- Only twenty matters per day as per their priority in the ballot are allowed to be raised on a day. However, 4 to 5 notices over and above these twenty matters of national/international importance could also be raised in the House, for which no ballot is held.
- These are allowed only at the discretion of Speaker.
- The order in which the matters will be raised, is decided by the Speaker, Lok Sabha.
- Just like in Lok Sabha, matters of urgent public importance can be raised with permission of the Chair in Rajya Sabha. This is on day to day basis..In Rajya Sabha, members can give notices for 'Zero Hour' from 12 Noon to 5 PM on the day prior to the day on which Members desire to raise their matters in the House.
- There are no provisions in Rules regarding Zero Hour.
- Only one matter on one subject can be raised by member.
- **Timeline**: Member seeking to raise matter under Zero Hour has to give notice upto 10 am on the day member wishes to raise.

- Government may or may not respond to matter raised under Zero Hour, just as in Lok Sabha.
- **The matters under Rule 377 in Lok Sabha and Special Mentions in Rajya Sabha and matters under ' Zero Hour ',are very popular among members particularly the backbenchers.**

Questions of Privilege

This apart a member can always raise a question of privilege under Rule 222 of the Lok Sabha Rules. There is no timeline for giving a notice of question of privilege. The notice of question of privilege can be given by a member at any time irrespective of the fact whether there is session or not.

The question of privilege raised by member remains alive till it is disposed off that is either it is disallowed, or Privileges Committee gives its report and action, if any, is taken by the House on the basis of recommendations made by the Committee in its report.

In Rajya Sabha, a privilege issue through a notice under Rule 187 can be raised by any member. A privilege issue can be issued on any day irrespective of whether there is session or not. Like in Lok Sabha, the privilege issue remains alive till a decision is taken thereon.

Rest of the procedure is broadly akin to that being followed in Lok Sabha.

It would be pertinent to briefly dwell upon parliamentary devices in Parliament of UK .

Position in UK

1. A *Committal Motion* is a proposal that a Bill should next be considered by a committee.
2. A 'Motion of Censure ' is one that seeks to criticise the

behaviour of the government: typically, the motion is critical of a specific government policy, or of the conduct of particular government minister.

3. A *Motion of No Confidence* is a motion moved in the House of Commons expressing lack of confidence in the government or a specific minister.
4. *Early Day Motions* (EDMs) are used by MPs in the Commons to draw the attention of the House to a particular issue, event or campaign. Other MPs may show their support for an EDM by adding their own signature to it.
5. *Motion to take Note* - A procedure used in the House of Lords to debate a subject without needing to take a specific decision. Motions to take note always begin "That this House takes note of ..." The debate may be on any subject, but the motion must be phrased in neutral terms (although members may give their opinions in the debate).
6. *Prayer Motion* - A prayer motion can be used by members of either House to object to a statutory instrument (SI). A motion seeking to overturn a negative instrument will include the wording: 'That a humble Address be presented to His Majesty, praying that [the instrument] be annulled'. In the Commons, such motions are usually tabled as an Early Day Motion. Other wordings can express regret over a particular aspect of the SI but will not stop the law taking effect.
7. *Non Fatal Motion* - A non-fatal motion does not stop a SI being law but may be used by either House to indicate concern. In the Commons, a prayer motion tabled outside the 40 sitting days period is non-fatal as it can only object to the SI, rather than stop it. The

most common non-fatal motion in the Lords is a motion to regret.

8. *Motion to Regret-* When the Lords considers a statutory instrument (SI), any member can introduce a motion to regret it. The motion usually gives specific reasons for the regret. Even if agreed, the motion cannot stop or amend the SI, but gives members an opportunity to put on record their dissent.

9. An *Oral Question* is a parliamentary questions that is put to a government minister in person by an MP or member of the House of Lords in the Chamber of each House. Oral question times to ministers normally take place at the beginning of each sitting day in both Houses on Mondays to Thursdays.

10. *Written Questions* are parliamentary questions that are put to government ministers in writing by MPs or Members of the Lords and that receive a written answer. These questions and answers are published online in the Written Questions and Answers database.

11. *Prime Minister's Question Time* (PMQ's) The Prime Minister answers questions from MPs in the House of Commons every sitting Wednesday from 12.00pm until the end of Question Time at 12.30pm.

12. *Business Questions* are the oral questions to the Leader of the House that MPs are allowed to ask, directly after the Leader has announced the forthcoming business in the House of Commons, each week on a Thursday. They are often used by MPs to ask the Government to make time for a debate on a specific issue.

13. *Private Notices Question* (PNQ) - A private notice question (PNQ) gives a member of the House of Lords the opportunity to ask an urgent and

important question to the government on any sitting day. A member of the Lords can apply to the Lord Speaker for a PNQ. If the Lord Speaker accepts the request, a government minister or spokesperson must come to the House of Lords Chamber and give an immediate answer without prior notice. During hybrid proceedings, the answer must be provided the following sitting day.Questions that are selected must be: related to a very recent or imminent event or development, important in terms of public policy, have more than a local or temporary significance. PNQs are asked immediately after oral questions on Monday to Thursday, or at an agreed time if on a Friday.

14. An *urgent question* requires a government minister to come to the House of Commons Chamber and give an immediate answer without prior notice. An MP can apply to the Speaker for an urgent question if they think a matter is urgent and important, and there is unlikely to be another way of raising it in the House. If the Speaker agrees, the question is asked at the end of that day's question time.

15. An *adjournment motion* is literally a motion: 'That this House (or sitting) do now adjourn'. In the Commons, however, debates on adjournment motions have covered almost every imaginable topic. This is because they have conventionally been used as a device to enable the House to discuss a particular issue in general terms and without needing to make a specific decision at the end.

16. *Private Members' Bills or Backbench Bills* - are introduced by individual MPs or members of the Lords rather than by the Government. As with other Public Bills

their purpose is to change the law as it applies to the general population. Very few Private Members' Bills become law but, by creating publicity around an issue, they may affect legislation indirectly.

17. *Questions for Short Debate* - In the House of Lords a Member may ask a question at the end of the day's business, or during the dinner break, and allow a short debate ending with a government reply. These were called 'unstarred questions' prior to the 2006-07 session.

18. *Supplementary Questions* are the follow-up oral questions that may be asked, without prior notice, during ministerial question sessions in both Houses. After a government minister has given a prepared answer to a question that they have been given notice of in advance, there is normally an opportunity for one or more further questions to be asked on the same topic.

19. *Topical Questions* in the House of Commons are questions that may be asked by MPs during the last 15 minutes of most ministerial question sessions. They allow MPs to ask a minister about anything they have responsibility for without having to give them advance notice of the question. In the House of Lords one topical question is asked at the end of most daily question sessions. Time is also allocated each Thursday for a topical question for short debate in the Lords.

20. *Ten Minute Rule Bills* are a type of Private Members' Bill that are introduced in the House of Commons under Standing Order No 23. The ten minute rule allows a backbench MP to make her or his case for a new Bill in a speech lasting up to ten minutes. An

opposing speech may also be made before the House decides whether or not the Bill should be introduced. If the MP is successful the Bill is taken to have had its first reading.

General – Reverting to procedural devices in Indian Parliament

Other than aforementioned procedural devices during Budget Session, members have opportunity to raise a wide range of issues during discussion on Motion of Thanks on President's Address and thereafter general discussion on Union Budget.

Relative importance of procedural devices

It would be important to note and be apprised of as to which procedural device can be optimally utilized to raise a particular issue:

Urgent topical matter on same day

- Adjournment motion under Rule 56 in Lok Sabha and notice for suspension of Rules under Rule 267 in Rajya Sabha.

Matter of urgent public importance

- Calling Attention under Rule 197 in Lok Sabha and Rule 180 [this has cushion time of one week and] can be raised by one or few members on statement made by Minister in regard to Calling Attention, members can seek clarification. Through this device important matter can be raised in House in just about 40 to 45 minutes or so normally.

Matter of public importance flagging usually a specific instance

- Matters under Rule 377 in Lok Sabha.
- Special Mentions under Rule 180A in Rajya Sabha.

[Has a cushion time of one week, member can raise constituency specific issue or relating to her/his constituents. Member subsequently gets written reply from the concerned Minister]

- Notices under Zero Hour on a day to day basis in both Houses.

[This enables members to raise a matter of public importance in the shortest possible time.]

Matter of public importance seeking discussion

- Short Duration Discussion, under Rule 193 in Lok Sabha and Rule 176 in Rajya Sabha.

[Though termed short duration discussion, but these devices enable detailed discussion, more members can participate. Minister replies at the end of debate but there is no voting]

Motions

Motion under Rule 184 in Lok Sabha and Rule 167 in Rajya Sabha.

This entails voting also after end of debate.

Conclusion

Procedural devices are well laid down in Rules of Procedure and Conduct of Business in Lok Sabha. Experience has shown members of Parliament have by and large very effectively utilised the procedural devices for raising matters of urgent public importance. There have been innovations too like firstly Calling Attention Motions and thereafter notices raised under Rule 377 in Lol Sabha and as Special Mentions in Rajya Sabha. Finally other procedural innovation that is matters that can be raised under 'Zero Hour'. All these have benefitted members cutting cross the party lines, to gainfully raise matters of public interest quite frequently in both Houses of Parliament.

••

6

BUDGET – Basic facts & budgetary terminology

It would be of interest to note some basic facts relating to budgetary process.

Origin

BUDGET is a popular word, not just in parliamentary parlance but is found in everyday use across the country indicating financial management. It's origin can be traced to late Middle English period from old French word "bougette", a diminutive of bonge a 'Leather bag' from Latin bulga, a Leather bag, knapsack of Gaulish origin. Elsewhere origin of the term budget has been traced to early 15th century to the word bouget meaning leather bag, wallet, pouch. In the mid-18th century, the Chancellor of the Exchequer, in the British House of Commons, in presenting his annual statement was said to 'open the budget'. In the late 19th Century, the use of the term was extended from government to other finances.

In India, the tradition adopted was the Finance Minister would carry the Budget proposals to Parliament in a new briefcase. This convention continued till a few years ago when Finance Minister of the National Democratic Alliance Government in 2014 carried the speech in a bag wrapped in a Red Colour. This move was interpreted as symbolic of Indian practice of 'Bahi Khata', a traditional book keeping register with a red-colour cover. This too has made way to the modern tablet that reinforces Parliament's march towards adaptation of paperless and digital work system.

Position in India

In the Constitution of India, the term Budget is not mentioned, instead under Article 112 the term used is "Annual Financial Statement". It states that the President shall in respect of every financial year cause to be laid before both the Houses of Parliament a statement of the estimated receipts and expenditure of the Government of India for that year and it has been referred to as the Annual Financial Statement in the said article. The term Budget has been taken as a synonym for "Annual Financial Statement".

However, 'Budget' finds mention in Rules of Procedure and Conduct of Business in Lok Sabha in Chapter XIX-Financial Business-Budget and the in the Rules of Procedure and Conduct of Business in the Council of States (Rajya Sabha) in Chapter XV.

Presentation of Budget

Till 2016, the Budget was presented to Lok Sabha in two parts, the Railway Budget pertaining to Railway Finance and the General Budget which presents an overall picture of the financial position of the Government of India, excluding the Railways. Since the financial year 2017-18, Railway Budget was merged or subsumed with the General

Budget, and now a single document titled 'Union Budget' is presented by the Minister of Finance.

Timings of Presentation of Budget

The practice of presentation of Budget at 1700 hours that began in the colonial period was on account of the time difference between New Delhi and Westminster, United Kingdom. The Indian time/zone is Four Hours 30 Minutes ahead of British Summer Time. The practice of presenting the Budget proposals in the evening meant that it was in time when the day began in London.

During National Democratic Alliance Government of Prime Minister Atal Bihari Vajpayee, the then Finance Minister Yashwant Sinha suggested the time be advanced to 1100 hours, the time when both Houses of Parliament commence sitting instead of the practice since British India. Among other reasons, the rationale behind the change in timing was that it could lead to better analysis of the announcements, numbers and provide ample time for an informed debate on the budget.

After consultations within the government and with stake holders, Finance Minister Sinha wrote to the Speaker of Lok Sabha and the Chairman of Rajya Sabha to drop the tradition of Question Hour on the day and thus on for the first time in the history of Indian Parliament, Budget was presented at 1100 hours on February 27, 1999 (28 February, 1999 being a Sunday).

This practice too underwent a change when the Budget during 2017-18 was presented on February1. The purpose was to ensure completion of the process of passage of the Budget before the end of the financial year so that the new proposals could be implemented from April 1, the start of a new financial year.

Constitutional Provisions

The passage of Budget is an elaborate stage by stage process. In fact, the provisions relating to budgetary process are laid down in Constitution itself. These are under various provisions.

- Article 112 – Annual Financial Statement
- Article 113 – Demands for Grants
- Article 114 – Appropriation Bill
- Article 115 – Supplementary additional or excess grants
- Article 116 – Vote on Account

These are to be read with relevant provisions in Rules of Procedure.

Various stages of Budgetary process

The various stages of Budget and its passage, termed Budgetary Process can be broadly classified as under:

- Presentation of Budget
- General discussion on Union Budget
- Consideration of Demands for Grants after presentation of Reports by Departmentally Related Standing Committees
- Discussion on Demands for Grants
- Cut Motions - Disapproval of Policy cut, Economy cut and Token cut
- Guillotine
- Vote on Account
- Supplementary and Excess Demands for Grants
- Appropriation Bill
- Finance Bill

The budgetary process ends with passage of Finance Bill.

The Budget Session is in two parts. Part-I of the Budget Session commences with address of the President of India to Members of both Houses of Parliament assembled together in the Central Hall (From February 1, 2024, President's Address is being held in Lok Sabha Chamber, new Parliament House). The next day the Budget is presented and Finance Bill is also introduced. Thereafter, for two or three days, there is discussion on Motion of Thanks on President's Address which is replied to by the Prime Minister of India. This is followed by General Discussion on Union Budget which also lasts for two or three days and at the end, the Minister of Finance replies to the debate. The Part-I of the Budget Session is usually for ten days or so. Thereafter, there is a recess of almost one month. During this period, Demands for Grants in the respect of various Ministries are examined by concerned Department Related Parliamentary Committees. In Part-II, the Department Related Standing Committees present their reports on Demands for Grants. Demands of some selected Ministries as decided by the Business Advisory Committee, Lok Sabha and these reports are discussed and adopted. On an appointed day, all the outstanding Demands for Grants are guillotined. This is followed by passage of Appropriation Bill in respect of Demands for Grants. Thereafter, the Finance Bill, which is a Money Bill, is taken up and discussed and passed. The procedure in respect of Finance Bill is the same as in case of other Money Bills.

Budget Terminology

In the context of passage of budget, several budget related terms are used. In a nutshell, the following broadly comprise of budget terminology:-

- Budget Estimates
- Revised Estimates
- Capital receipts

- Capital expenditures
- Revenue receipts
- Revenue (or Committed) expenditure
- Voted Expenditure
- Charged Expenditure
- Fiscal Deficit
- Primary Deficit
- Revenue Deficit
- Trade Deficit
- Effective Revenue Deficit
- Direct Tax
- Indirect Tax
- Corporate tax
- Ad Valorem Tax
- Countervailing Duties (CVD)
- Wholesale Price Index (WPI)
- Consumer Price Index (CPI)
- Base Effect
- Monetary Policy
- Fiscal Consolidation
- Consolidated Fund of India (Article 266)
- Contingency Fund
- Public Account
- Demands for Grants {Article 113(2)}
- Supplementary Demands for Grants {Article 115}
- Central Plan Outlays
- Central Sector Scheme
- Centrally Sponsored Schemes
- Guillotine
- Cut Motion
- Appropriation Bill {Appropriation bills as provided for under Article 114 is a Money Bill in terms of Article 110}

- Finance Bill {This is a Money Bill in terms of provisions of Article 110}

The Budgetary process is a very complex and involves various procedural stages. The thrust of the present article is to give only a broad idea about the passage of the Budget expressed in simple terms.

●●

7

No-Confidence Motion— A Broad Overview

Motion of No-Confidence in the Council of Ministers

A motion of No-Confidence the most potent parliamentary device can be moved only in Lok Sabha.

One of the fundamental postulates of parliamentary democracy is the principle of collective responsibility of the Council of Ministers headed by the Prime Minister, to Lok Sabha – the House of People. This responsibility is joint and indivisible. Collective Ministerial responsibility of the House of People (Lok Sabha) is the crux of parliamentary democracy in India. Article 75(3) of the Constitution of India provides that "The Council of Ministers shall be collectively responsible to the House of People". The Council of Ministers must enjoy the confidence of the House of People to stay in power. Whenever there emerges a situation, when it is perceived that the Government (Party in power) does not enjoy majority support, the well established procedural device of motion of no-confidence under Rule 198(1) of the Rules of Procedure and Conduct of Business in Lok Sabha, is taken recourse to, to test the majority of the Government of the day. Hence, a No Confidence Motion can be raised only in the Lok Sabha. Moving of a No-Confidence could be termed as device (weapon) of last resort when section of Members/Members of Lok Sabha move against the Government, which is indicative of lack of trust in the Government, the ruling dispensation.

In this context, it would be worthwhile to take note of text Article 75(3) of the Constitution which provides that "The Council of Ministers shall be collectively responsible to the House of People".

In interpreting Article 75(3), the Supreme Court of India in U.N.R. Rao vs. Smt. Indira Gandhi (A.I.R. 1971, SC) observed:-

"Article 75(3) brings into existence what is usually called 'Responsible Government'. In other words the Council of Ministers must enjoy the confidence of the House of the People. While the House of the People is not dissolved under art. 85(2)(b), art 73(3) has full operation. But when it is dissolved, the Council of Ministers cannot naturally enjoy the confidence of the House of the People... Art. 75(3) only applies when the House of the People does not stand dissolved."

The provisions for moving a No-Confidence Motion are provided for in Rule 198 of the Rules of Procedure and Conduct of Business in Lok Sabha.

The procedure for moving a No-Confidence Motion is explained briefly as under:-

A motion expressing want of confidence in the Council of Ministers may be made subject to the following restrictions:-

(a) leave to make the motion shall be asked for by the Member when called by the Speaker;

(b) the Member asking for leave shall by 10.00 hours on that day give to the Secretary-General a written notice of the motion which such member proposes to move.

As per proviso to this Rule, notices received after 10.00 hrs on a day shall be deemed to have been received at 10.00 hrs on the next day on which the House sits.

If the Speaker is of the opinion that the motion is in order, the Speaker shall read the motion to the House and shall request those members who are in favour of leave being granted to rise in their places, and if not less than fifty members rise accordingly, the Speaker shall declare that leave is granted and that the motion will be taken up on such day, not being more than ten days from the date on which the leave is asked for as the Speaker may appoint. If less than fifty members rise, the Speaker shall inform that the member has not the leave of the House. In case number of notices of No-Confidence Motion are received for the same sitting, the notices are balloted to determine their *inter se* priority. Notices which are held to be in order are taken up one-by-one in the order of their priority. In case leave of the House, first Motion is granted then all other Motions become infructuous. On the other hand, if leave of the House for moving the first Motion is not granted, the second Motion is taken up, so on and so forth.

If leave is granted, the Speaker may, after considering the state of business in the House, allot a day or days or part of a day for the discussion of the motion. A Motion so admitted has to be listed for discussion on a day not exceeding 10 days from the day the Motion has been admitted. While it is not as such specified, the mode of computation of the 10 days, it is settled practice that in computing the 10 days the Session days/working days of Parliament alone are considered. Meaning thereby the intervening weekend or weekends, closed holidays and parliamentary holidays are not taken into account.

It is well established that "When leave of the House to the moving of a motion has been granted, no substantive motion on policy matters is to be brought before the House by the Government till the motion of no-confidence has been disposed of". [Practice and Procedure of Parliament by M. N. Kaul & S. L. Shakdher, 7th Edn., p. 772, Lok Sabha Debates dated 25-7-1966, c. 230; 26-7-1966, c. 457; 27-7-1966. c. 777; 24-7-1974, c. 221]

Thereafter, the Speaker shall, at the appointed hour on the allotted day or the last of the allotted days, as the case may be, forthwith put every question necessary to determine the decision of the House on the motion.

The Speaker, if thinks fit, may prescribe a time limit for speeches.

A No-Confidence Motion is distinct from censure motion. A motion of No-Confidence need not set out any ground or charges on which it is based. The grounds do not form part of the motion. The standard format of No-Confidence Motion is "That this House expresses its confidence in the Council of Ministers".

Once a motion of No-Confidence Motion is adopted, the Government of the day has to resign as it clearly indicates that the Government does not enjoy the confidence/the requisite majority to govern.

No-Confidence Motions discussed so far

It was during the third Lok Sabha in 1963 that the first motion of no confidence was moved by Acharya J B Kripalani against the government headed by Prime Minister Jawaharlal Nehru. The debate on the motion lasted for 21 hours over four days, with 40 MPs participating. This No-Confidence Motion was defeated.

Till date, Motions of No-Confidence had been discussed in Lok Sabha on 28 occasions. As a matter of fact, there had been 15 No-Confidence Motions against the Government headed by Smt. Indira Gandhi. All these Motions were defeated. **However in this context it would of interest to take note of three instances when Governments fell on defeat of Confidence Motions brought by Prime Ministers** as per the details given below:-

1. Against Shri V. P. Singh's Government

    Shri VP Singh was a member of the Janata Dal party and held the office of Prime Minister from 1989 to 1990. He headed a coalition government called the National Front, which was supported by the BJP. His government lost **Confidence Motion** after the BJP had withdrawn its support over the Ram Temple issue. He lost the motion by 142 votes to 346 votes.

2. Against Shri H. D. Deve Gowda's Government

    Deve Gowda of Janata Dal became the Prime Minister in 1996, with a coalition known as the United Front with the support of Congress. However, Congress withdrew their support a few months later and Gowda's government **brought forward a Confidence Motion**. The motion was moved on April 11, 1997, and the Gowda government could garner only 158 votes, thus losing the motion.

3. Against Shri Atal Bihari Vajpayee's Government

    The BJP stalwart, who first became the Prime Minister in 1996, had lost the first **Confidence Motion** by just a single vote in 1999 after Jayalalitha-led AIADMK withdrew support. Subsequently, a no-confidence motion was brought against Shri Vajpayee's Government in 2003, which he won by an overwhelming majority.

    It is the Prime Minister being the head of the

Government replies to the debate on No-Confidence Motion. There have, however, been two exceptions to the settled practice. In 6th Lok Sabha, a notice of No-Confidence Motion was given by Shri Y. B. Chavan from INC against Janata Party Government headed by Shri Morarji Desai. This No-Confidence Motion was discussed on July 12, 1979. However, the discussion remained inconclusive as Shri Morarji Desai tendered his resignation before the Motion could be put to vote. In 7th Lok Sabha, a notice of No-Confidence Motion was given by Shri George Fernandes against Government headed by Smt. Indira Gandhi. When the notice was given, the Prime Minister was on the official nine day tour. The then government were of the view that this Motion could be discussed after return of Smt. Indira Gandhi, the then Prime Minister from her pre-scheduled official tour. The Opposition, however, did not agree. Under these circumstances, the reply to the No-Confidence Motion was given by Shri R. Venkatraman on 9 May, 1981. This Motion was defeated.

A list of No-Confidence Motions discussed till date is as below:-

The thrust of the article is to give an overall perspective of the most powerful parliamentary device *i.e.* No-Confidence Motion.

Sl. No.	Mover	Prime Minister	Date of Voting	Members Participated	Prime Minister replied
1	Shri J.B. Kripalani	Shri Jawaharlal Nehru	22.8.63	44	YES
2	Shri N.C. Chatterjee	Shri Lal Bahadur Shastri	18.9.64	57	YES

3	Shri S.N. Dwivedy	Shri Lal Bahadur Shastri	16.3.65	19	YES
4	Shri M.R. Masani	Shri Lal Bahadur Shastri	26.8.65	37	YES
5	Shri H.N. Mukherjee	Smt. Indira Gandhi	4.8.66	37	YES
6	Shri U.M. Trivedi	Smt. Indira Gandhi	7.11.66	29	YES
7	Shri A.B. Vajpayee- I	Smt. Indira Gandhi	20.3.67	23	YES
8	Shri Madhu Limaye- I	Smt. Indira Gandhi	24.11.67	26	YES
9	Shri Balraj Madhok	Smt. Indira Gandhi	28.2.68	20	YES
10	Shri K.L. Gupta	Smt. Indira Gandhi	13.11.68	22	YES
11	Shri P. Ramamurti	Smt. Indira Gandhi	20.2.69	26	YES
12	Shri Madhu Limaye- II	Smt. Indira Gandhi	29.7.70	29	YES
13	Shri Jyotirmoy Bosu-I	Smt. Indira Gandhi	22.11.73	19	YES
14	Shri Jyotirmoy Bosu-II	Smt. Indira Gandhi	10.5.74	31	YES
15	Shri Jyotirmoy Bosu-III	Smt. Indira Gandhi	25.7.74	25	YES
16	Shri Jyotirmoy Bosu-IV	Smt. Indira Gandhi	9.5.75	16	YES
17	Shri C.M. Stephen	Shri Morarji Desai	11.5.78	28	YES

18	Shri Y.B. Chavan	Shri Morarji Desai	12.7.79	23	Prime Minister was on an official nine-day tour
19	Shri George Fernandes	Smt. Indira Gandhi	9.5.81	21	Prime Minister was on an official nine-day tour
20	Shri Samar Mukherjee	Smt. Indira Gandhi	17.9.81	19	YES
21	Shri H.N. Bahuguna	Smt. Indira Gandhi	16.8.82	25	YES
22	Shri C. Madhav Reddy	Shri Rajiv Gandhi	11.12.87	22	YES
23	Shri Jaswant Singh	Shri Narasimha Rao	17.7.92	24	YES
24	Shri A.B. Vajpayee- I	Shri Narasimha Rao	21.12.92	57	YES
25	Shri Ajoy Mukhopadhyay	Narasimha Rao	28.7.93	30	YES
26	Smt. Sonia Gandhi	Shri A.B. Vajpayee	19.8.2003	39	YES
27	Shri Srinivas Kesineni	Shri Narendra Modi	20.07.2018	51	YES
28	Shri Gaurav Gogoi	Shri Narendra Modi	10.08.2023	79	YES

8

Status of Members Expelled from Political Parties

The issue of expulsion of members from their primary membership of the party and their status is a delicate matter. This article seeks to put forth the legal position.

Political parties play a pivotal role in a democratic polity. Political parties have always been integral to functioning of democratic systems world over and so is in India.

In the context of importance of political parties, it would be worth noting the following observations made by Sir Ivor Jennings in his book "Cabinet Government" (3rd Edition, 1969, pp 473-474)

"The successful candidate is almost invariably returned to Parliament, not because of his personality nor because of his judgement and capacity, but because of his party label... He (candidate) possesses an organization because the party supporters in the locality-stimulated, if necessary by the party headquarters-believe in the party affiliation sufficiently strongly to give time and trouble to its work."

One of the characteristic features of Indian polity is the pre dominance of political pluralism.

With the coming into force of the Tenth Schedule to the Constitution of India (Anti-Defection Law) insofar as members of either House of Parliament or State Legislatures are concerned, under the provisions of Tenth Schedule to the Constitution, they can be categorized only in either of these three categories, i.e., (1) as belonging to a Legislature Party; (2) Independent Member; or (3) Nominated Member. There are no provisions *vis-à-vis* expulsion of members from their political parties.

Expulsion as one of the grounds of defections (as originally provided)

The Constitution (Fifty-Second Amendment) Bill,1985 introduced in Lok Sabha on January 24, 1985 which sought to incorporate Tenth Schedule to the Constitution (Anti-Defection Law), also provided for expulsion from political party as one of the grounds for disqualification from membership of the House.

However, in view of concerns expressed by members cutting across the party lines in deference to the predominant view that emerged, Rajiv Gandhi Government decided to exclude this provision, i.e., expulsion as one of the grounds for defection from the Constitution (Fifty-Second Amendment) Bill.

Consequences of expulsion of member from political party

It is well settled that a political party has disciplinary control over its members and may expel a member under the provisions of the concerned Party's Constitution.

Prior to the coming into force of the Constitution

(Fifty-Second Amendment) Act, 1985, and the rules framed thereunder, the established practice in Lok Sabha has been that if a member of a political party was expelled from his party, he was treated as unattached in the House. The Constitution (Fifty-Second Amendment) Act, 1985, and the rules framed thereunder do not make provision for a situation arising out of a member's expulsion from his political party for his activities outside the House. Hence, the Act and the rules do not stipulate the existence of an unattached member.

A similar approach was adopted during Ninth Lok Sabha when the then Speaker (Shri Rabi Ray) declared 25 members expelled from the Janata Dal, as unattached.

During Tenth Lok Sabha, however, the then Speaker (Shri Shivraj V. Patil) in his decision in the Janata Dal case adopted a different approach and observed as follows:-

"In the past, in some cases, when the Members were expelled, they were called Unattached, to distinguish them from the party Members as well as from the independent Member. The word Unattached is not used anywhere in the Tenth Schedule or any part of the Constitution of India or any other relevant laws or the Rules of Procedure followed in the Parliament." (paras 88 & 89 of the decision in the Janata Dal case dated 1.6.1993)

In the same decision, Speaker (Shri Patil) took a view [Decision in Janata Dal case given by the Speaker, 10th Lok Sabha on 1.6.1993 (paras 81, 83-84)] that it is doubtful that expulsion from a political party would automatically result in expulsion of the member from the Legislature party as well.

In this context, it would be of interest to note the observations made by the Supreme Court of India in **G. Viswanathan Vs. Speaker, Tamil Nadu Legislative**

Assembly and Azhagu Thirunavakkarasu Vs. Speaker, Tamil Nadu Legislative Assembly cases [(1996)2 Supreme Court cases 353]. [1996 AIR 1060]

The Hon'ble Court *inter alia* held as follows:-

"Even if a member is thrown out or expelled from the party, for the purposes of the Tenth Schedule he will not cease to be a member of the political party that had set him up as a candidate for the election. He will continue to belong to that political party even if he is treated as 'unattached'."

Halim Committee Report

A Committee of Presiding Officers of Legislative Bodies in India on the need to review the Anti-Defection Law under the Chairmanship of Shri Hashim Abdul Halim, the then Speaker, West Bengal Legislative Assembly was constituted on 13 October, 1998. The Committee was reconstituted on 26 July, 2001 and 18 July, 2002. The Committee presented their Report at the 66th Conference of Presiding Officers at Mumbai on 5 February, 2003. The Committee in their Report pointed out that there was a significant incongruity in the Anti-Defection Law in as much as that there was no provision to cope with situations arising out of expulsions of members. The Committee felt that the status of the expellees should be clearly spelt out in the Anti-Defection Law. [Report of the Committee of the Presiding Officers of the Legislative Bodies on "A Review of Anti-Defection Law" (paras 3.9 to 3.22)]

Conclusion

As already discussed, the Tenth Schedule to the Constitution does not contain any provisions *vis-à-vis* the status of expelled members. However, the Supreme Court of India in their decided cases (G. Viswanathan Vs. Speaker,

Tamil Nadu Legislative Assembly-in G. Viswanathan case in 1996 later reiterated, in Jagjit Singh case in 2004) have clearly laid down that expulsion of a member from political party would not in any way affect her or his membership of either House of Parliament or State Legislature, as the case may be.

••

9

Understanding White Papers: A Brief Overview

White Papers play a vital role in policymaking, providing a foundation for discussion, informing decision-makers, and guiding future actions.

In an era where information is both a tool and a weapon, the concept of a white paper has emerged as a beacon of clarity, particularly in the complex world of governance. On February 8, 2024, Finance Minister Nirmala Sitharaman presented a pivotal white paper on the Indian economy in Parliament, spotlighting the financial narrative that has unfolded over the past two decades. This document, prepared by the Ministry of Finance, embarked on a comparative journey, evaluating the 10-year economic stewardship of the Congress-led United Progressive Alliance (UPA) governments from 2004-05 to 2013-14 against the subsequent decade under the Bharatiya Janata Party (BJP)-led National Democratic Alliance (NDA) governments from 2014-15 to 2023-24.

Amidst this backdrop, it is imperative to demystify what a "white paper" entails. Originating from the British government, the term was coined to distinguish these policy documents from other forms of government publications, such as green papers (more exploratory documents inviting discussion) or blue books (detailed reports or collections of statistics). The historical roots of white papers trace back to 1922 with the Churchill White Paper, also known as the "British Policy in Palestine," introduced by Winston Churchill. This document set a precedent for governments worldwide to use white papers as a strategic tool for articulating positions, addressing public concerns, and enhancing transparency.

A white paper in the parliamentary context serves as a comprehensive report or guide informing stakeholders about complex issues and offering insight into government policies or proposed legislation. These documents play a vital role in policymaking, providing a foundation for discussion, informing decision-makers, and guiding future actions. They are instrumental for legislators, policymakers, researchers, and the public, offering a platform for understanding and debating significant issues or developing new policies.

The essence of white papers extend beyond merely informing. They are designed to dissect intricate topics into digestible segments, allowing stakeholders to comprehend the nuances of an issue and formulate their strategies. While suggestive in nature, white papers invite opinions, discussions, and feedback, facilitating a more inclusive approach to policy formulation and legislative changes.

The flexibility in the issuance of white papers by governments underscores the adaptability of this tool. Without stringent guidelines or timelines, governments can issue white papers on pertinent topics at any time, reflecting the dynamic nature of governance and policy development. This flexibility also extends to the opposition, which can demand white papers on contentious issues, adding a layer of accountability and transparency to the governance process.

Illustrative of their significant impact, white papers have been instrumental in addressing and discussing various national concerns. Notably, a White Paper on the 'Punjab Agitation' was laid and debated in Parliament in July 1984, and a 'White Paper on Black Money' was presented in 2012, reflecting the government's stance on critical issues and inviting public discourse.

The presentation of the white paper on the Indian economy by Finance Minister Nirmala Sitharaman serves as a contemporary example of this tradition, seeking to offer an analysis of economic governance over the past two decades. By comparing the economic records of the UPA and NDA governments, this document sought to provide a basis for assessing policy effectiveness.

In essence, white papers serve as a conduct for transparent governance. They empower governments to articulate policies, address public concerns, and foster a culture of trust. As dynamic tools for communication, white papers significantly influence public discourse, enhance accountability, and promote informed decision-making. In the realms of governance, business, and academia, they remain indispensable for clarifying complex issues, shaping policy debates, and guiding societal progress. The role of white papers is to foster an informed and engaged citizenry underpinning their enduring value in the tapestry of democratic governance.

••

10

Marriage Equality and 17 October, 2013 Supreme Court Verdict– An Overview

Same-sex marriages has been an emotive issue world over and India is no exception to that. While in India the issues of gay rights, same sex marriages had been being raised by queer unions for sometime now, the matter came to fore with recent Supreme Court judgement in October.

Earlier in April, the Supreme Court said it would not get involved in personal laws. Instead, it would focus on looking at whether the Special Marriage Act of 1954 could include the right to marry for LGBTQ+ couples.

A **five-judge Bench** of the Supreme Court on Tuesday, October 17, 2013 announced a **3:2 verdict** on petitions seeking the rights for members of the LGBTQ community to marry and choose family.

The Supreme Court on October 17, 2023 refused to allow same-sex marriages in India even as it directed the government to set up a high-powered committee headed by the Cabinet Secretary to decide the rights and entitlements of persons in queer unions.

A five-judge Constitution Bench headed by the Chief Justice of India DY Chandrachud refused to grant legal recognition to same-sex marriages.

There were four verdicts – one each by CJI Chandrachud, Justice Sanjay Kishan Kaul, Justice S Ravindra Bhat and Justice PS Narasimha.

The majority judgement was given by Justice Narasimha, Justice S. Ravindra Bhat and Justice Hima Kohli.

Highlights of the Majority Judgement: Justice Narasimha, Justice S Ravindra Bhat and Justice Hima Kohli

- All the judges were unanimous in holding that there is no unqualified right to marriage and that same-sex couples cannot claim it as a fundamental right.
- The Court also unanimously turned down the challenge to provisions of the Special Marriage Act.
- The majority of Justices Bhat, Kohli and Narasimha also held that civil unions between same sex couples are not recognised under law and they cannot claim the right to adopt children either.
- Entitlement to legal recognition of the right to civil union akin to marriage or conferring status upon the parties to the relationship can be only through enacted law. The Court cannot enjoin or direct the creation of such regulatory framework resulting in such legal status.
- Queer couples have the right to union or relationship be it mental, emotional or sexual, drawing from the right to privacy, the right to choice and the right to autonomy. This does not, however, give them the

right to claim legal status or entitlement to the said union.
- Challenge to the Special Marriage Act insofar as it does not recognize unions between same-sex couples, is dismissed.
- The Central government should be set up a high-powered committee (HPC) chaired by the Cabinet Secretary to undertake a comprehensive examination of all relevant factors related to same-sex marriage.
- The HPC shall take into account views of all stakeholders and all states and union territories.
- Transgenders persons in heterosexual relationships have the freedom and entitlement to marry.

Highlights of the Minority Judgement: Chief Justice Chandrachud and Justice SK Kaul

- The minority decision of a Supreme Court Constitution Bench on Tuesday recognized the right of same-sex couples to enter into a civil union.
- Chief Justice of India (CJI) DY Chandrachud and Justice Sanjay Kishan Kauldis agreed with the majority decision to not recognize the right of same-sex couples to enter into marriages or have civil unions.
- "The right to enter into a union cannot be restricted based on sexual orientation. Such a restriction will be violative of Article 15. Thus, this freedom is available to all persons regardless of gender identity or sexual orientation," they said.
- The CJI and Justice Kaul, however, also ruled that it would be within the domain of Parliament to give legal recognition to same-sex marriages.
- The judges said that the State, by not endorsing a form

of relationship, was encouraging certain preferences over others.
- They opined that the failure of the State to recognize the entitlements that flow from a legalized marriage would result in a *"disparate impact on queer couples who cannot marry under the current legal regime"*.
- Holding the restriction against the union of queer couples on the basis of their sexual orientation to be violative of Article 15 of the Constitution, the judges said:

"The word 'sex' must be read to include sexual orientation, not only because of the causal relationship between homophobia and sexism, but also because the word 'sex' is used as a marker of identity, which cannot be read independent of the social and historical context."

- CJI Chandrachud and Justice Kaul further said that the decision in *Navtej Singh Johar v. Union of India* and the nine-judge Constitution Bench decision in *Justice KS Puttaswamy (Retd) & Anr v. Union of India & Ors* recognizes the right of couples to exercise the choice to enter into a union.
- They added that transgender persons in heterosexual relationships have the right to marry under existing law including personal laws which regulate marriage.
- The judges also said that the Central and state governments and the administrations of union territories shall not discriminate against the freedom of queer persons to enter into union with benefits under law.

An appraisal

After having taken note of the views expressed in majority and minority judgements by the Supreme Court, for the sake of better clarity point wise appraisal of the Supreme Court's judgement has been made as under:-

Previously, the decriminalization of Section 377 from the Indian Penal Code was a big step in the right direction, but it was just the beginning of a tough journey toward achieving full equality for LGBTQIA+ individuals.

The verdict in points:
- Same sex couples do not have a "right to marry©.
- Transgender persons have a right to marry under the current framework.
- Same-sex couples have a right to choose their partners and cohabit with one another.
- Queer couples do not have the right to adopt (3:2 verdict)
- Couples do not enjoy a right to a civil union (3:2 verdict)

Explanation:
- The verdict refused to afford legal recognition to same-sex marriages since marriage "as a social institution predates all rights, forms of political thought and laws," and there is no unqualified right to marry that people can claim as a fundamental right.
- **The Court also refused to strike down or read words to interpret the Special Marriage Act (SMA) as gender-neutral**: doing so would both infringe upon the legislature's role and have a "cascading" impact on other laws.
- The Bench affirmed that **people have a right to choose one's partners and to cohabit with one another**. "The capacity of non-heterosexual couples for love, commitment and responsibility is no less worthy of

regard than heterosexual couples. Let us preserve this autonomy, so long as it does not infringe on the rights of others," Justice Kaul said.
- **The disagreement centred on how far the law can go on matters of adoption rights and the right to form civil unions.** The majority opinions were held by Justices S. Ravindra Bhat, Hima Kohli and P.S. Narasimha, and the minority views by the Chief Justice and Justice S.K. Kaul.
- There was an **overall majority affirming that transpersons in heterosexual relationships have the "right to marry under the existing laws** or personal laws," and general consensus about the harassment and discrimination faced by people in queer relationships. **It directed the Union Government to form a high-powered committee to look into their concerns.**

On adoption rights
- The majority opinion **refused to strike down** the Central Adoption Resource Authority **(CARA) regulations that restrict queer couples from adopting a child**. The law is equipped to protect the child in case a heterosexual marriage ends or a partner dies, but there is no such framework for homosexual couples at present, the judgment states.
- The **CJI in his opinion noted that adoption regulations at present are discriminatory to the queer community** and violative of Article 14, adding that "marriage alone does not give stability to a household".
- The **majority view, however, ruled against adoption rights for same-sex couples.** In consensus with Justices

Narasimha and Kohli, Justice Ravindra Bhat said the regulations cannot be held unconstitutional but "This is not to say that unmarried or non-heterosexual couples can't be good parents". According to them, the State as a legal protector has to explore all areas and to ensure all benefits reach the children at large in need of stable homes.

On trans-persons' rights:
- The majoritarian opinion of the Bench being that **trans-persons have the right to marry under the existing framework formed since a transgender person can be in a heterosexual relationship.** "The gender of a person is not the same as their sexuality," the judgment noted.
- The Court affirmed the Madras High Court decision in *Arun Kumar v. Inspector General of Registration*, which declared marriage between a Hindu male and a transwoman a valid union.

Can States make their own laws?
- The decision raises the issue of marriage equality for lawmakers. Since there's no central law on this, the judgement says that state governments can make laws that recognize and regulate same-sex marriages. **The Constitution, under Articles 245 and 246, empowers both the Parliament and the State to enact marriage regulations.**

Directives by the Supreme Court are as under:-
- Ensuring that the queer community is not discriminated against because of gender identity or sexual orientation.

- Sensitising public about queer identity.
- Establishing hotline numbers the queer community can access.
- Establishing safe houses in all districts to provide shelter to members facing violence.
- A ban on treatments that aim to change gender identity or sexual orientation.
- Inter-sex children are not forced to undergo operations.
- No person shall be forced to undergo any hormonal therapy Ensure there is no discrimination in access to goods and services.
- The Mental Healthcare Act must formulate modules to safeguard mental health of queer persons and implement programmes to reduce suicides.

Directions given by the Supreme Court for the government

- Earlier the government dwelled on the "unnatural nature of queerness, arguing that homosexual unions are not innate, do not precede law and are non-Indian. The verdict debunks these to a degree, evoking the spirit of the 2018 ruling that "queer love has flourished in India since ancient times."
- The **Court called on the Solicitor General's submission that the government will constitute a committee**, chaired by the Cabinet Secretary, to set out the benefits and entitlements for same-sex couples.

The International Scenario:
- **There are 34 countries in the world where same-sex marriage is legal,** according to a Pew Research report.

- These are – Andorra, Argentina, Australia, Austria, Belgium, Brazil, Canada, Chile, Colombia, Costa Rica, Cuba, Denmark, Ecuador, Finland, France, Germany, Iceland, Ireland, Luxembourg, Malta, Mexico, the Netherlands, New Zealand, Norway, Portugal, Slovenia, South Africa, Spain, Sweden, Switzerland, Taiwan, the United Kingdom, the United States of America and Uruguay.
- The **Netherlands became the first country in 2001** and **Andorra (a European country) became the latest** nation to legalise same-sex marriages.
- Estonia's parliament passed on June 20, 2023, a law legalizing same-sex marriage that came into effect January 1, 2024.
- **Taiwan** gained international attention in 2019 by **being the first Asian nation to legalize** same-sex marriage.
- Similarly, **within the African continent, only South Africa** recognizes same-sex marriage. (Details may be seen at Annexure)

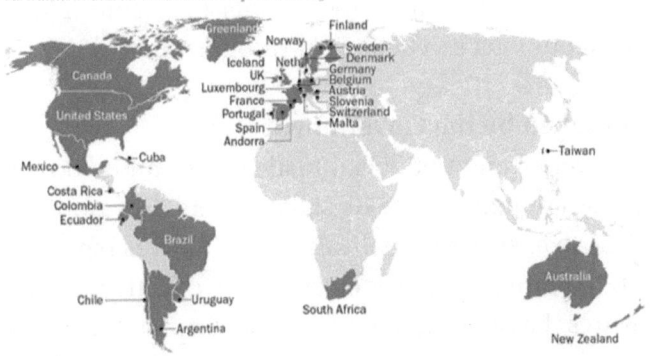

Same-sex marriage is legal in more than 30 places around the world – A snapshot view

Jurisdictions that allow same-sex couples to marry

Note: Classifications as of May 2023.
Source: Pew Research Center analysis of news articles and official government sources.
PEW RESEARCH CENTER

It may be noted that the Same-sex married couples in many countries do not share all of the same rights and benefits as different-sex married couples, such as the right to adoption. In some countries, same-sex couples also experience additional restrictions. For example, in Taiwan same-sex marriage is only available to Taiwanese citizens or a citizen of a foreign country that recognizes same- sex marriage who seeks to marry a Taiwanese citizen.

Methodology adopted internationally in legalizing same-sex marriages

- It's important to know that **the rules for same-sex couples to get a marriage license can be different.**
- For example, 23 countries have legalized same-sex marriage nationally through legislation.
- Among these, Australia, Ireland and Switzerland legalized same-sex marriage through legislation only after nation-wide votes.
- In United States of America, it was legalized as late as 2015.
- **10 countries have legalized same-sex marriage nationally through court** decisions.

The Supreme Court had accordingly placed upon the Parliament and State Governments to decide if non-heterosexual unions can be legally recognized.

Measures taken by the Government

The Department of Social Justice and Empowerment (DoSJE) has invited inputs of stakeholders and public at large, so as to ensure that policies and initiatives regarding LGBTQI+ community are inclusive and effective. A host of measures have been taken by Government of India regarding the community.

Government of India, through a gazette notification

dated April 16, 2024, constituted a Committee with Cabinet Secretary as the Chairperson and Secretaries of Ministry of Home Affairs, Ministry of Women and Child Development, Ministry of Health and Family Welfare, Legislative Department, as Members and Secretary, Department of Social Justice and Empowerment as Member Convenor to examine and submit recommendations on the measures to be taken by Central and State Governments to safeguard the interest of the queer community.

The Committee met on 21 May, 2024 to discuss issues relating to issue of ration cards, enabling individuals belonging to queer community to have joint bank account with option to name the partner as nominee, harassment on account of their gender identity, sexual orientation etc. It was also decided that a sub-committee be set up to further discuss and finalise the issues pertaining to ration cards, bank accounts, jail visitation requests, law and order measures to ensure that queer community do not face any threat of violence, harassment or coercion, etc.

The sub-committee met on May 31, 2024 under the chairmanship of the Home Secretary, Ministry of Home Affairs. The sub-committee discussed the measures to address discrimination that queer community face especially in relation to their access to social welfare benefits, healthcare and public goods services; police action and violence, etc and asked the Ministries/ Departments to prepare an OM/ advisory for issuance. Thereafter, Ministry of Home Affairs issued advisory to all states/UTs regarding prison visitation rights of the Queer Community and an advisory, on law & order measures to be taken to ensure that queer community do not face any threat of violence, harassment or coercion.

The Department of Social Justice and Empowerment held 'Consultation on LGBTQIA+ matters' on 25 July, 2024 with representative members from the LGBTQIA+ community, central Ministries and states. The inputs/suggestions received during the stakeholder consultations have been shared with concerned Ministries/Departments for examination and taking further steps.

The second meeting of Committee under the chairmanship of Cabinet Secretary met on August 22, 2024 and reviewed the status of action taken by Ministries/departments and directed them to immediately issue OMs/advisories pertaining to queer community.

Accordingly, Government of India has already taken following **interim action**:

i. Department of Food and Public Distribution (D/oF&PD) has issued an advisory to all the States and UTs, that as per existing provisions, enabling partners in a queer relationship are to be treated as a part of the same household for the purposes of ration card. Further, States/UTs have been asked to take necessary measures to ensure that partners in queer relationship are not subject to any discrimination in the issuance of ration cards.

ii. Department of Financial Services (DFS) has issued an advisory that there are no restrictions for persons of the queer community to open a joint bank account and also to nominate a person in queer relationship as a nominee to receive the balance in the account, in the event of death of the account holder.

iii. Ministry of Health and Family Welfare has issued letters to all stakeholders including all States/UTs to take measures to ensure the rights of LGBTQI+ community with relation to healthcare, planning awareness activities, prohibition of conversion therapy, availability of sex reassignment surgery, changes in curricula, provision of Tele consultation, sensitization and training various levels of staff and making of provision to claim the body when near relative/next of kin/family is not available.

iv. The Directorate General of Health Services, Ministry of Health and Family Welfare has also issued letter to the State Health Departments and other stakeholders on the subject of ensuring the health care access and reducing discrimination towards LGBTQI+ community.

v. Ministry of Health and Family Welfare has framed guidelines in respect of medical intervention required in infants/ children with disorders of sexual differentiation (intersex) to have medically normal life without complications. The Ministry is working on guidelines to address the issues pertaining to mental health/well-being of queer community.

The DoSJE has invited public to share their suggestions and feedback for further measures to be taken regarding queer communities. [Courtesy Press Release issued by Press Information Bureau, Government of India (Ministry of Social Justice & Empowerment)]

On August 28, 2024, the Department of Financial Services *vide* their Advisory No. F. No. 6/8/2024 – Welfare) confirmed the Reserve Bank of India's advisory allowing queer couples in India to open joint bank accounts and nominate partners, following the Supreme Court's 2022 ruling. However, the absence of clear guidelines for proof of relationship had led banks to adopt varied verification processes, creating challenges despite this progress.

Conclusion

Given the sensibility of the matter in this article no personal views have been expressed. The thrust of the article is to make aware the highlight the points made by the Supreme Court, the Apex Court of the land on the issue and the prevailing position in this regard world over and measures taken so far by Government of India in view of Supreme Court's judgement.

****

ANNEXURE
Legalization of Same-sex Marriage around the world

Sl.No.	Country	Year	Region	Notes
1	Netherlands	2001	Europe	First country to legalize same-sex marriage after Parliament passed the law in December 2000.
2	Belgium	2003	Europe	Second country in the world to legalize same-sex marriage, after its neighbor, the Netherlands.
3	Canada	2005	North America	Same-sex marriage was legal in a majority of Canada's provinces before Parliament passed national legislation.
4	Spain	2005	Europe	Became the third country globally to legalize same-sex marriage after a vote in its closely divided Parliament.
5	South Africa	2006	Sub-Saharan Africa	Only African country where same-sex marriage is legal; several countries on the continent have passed laws that ban homosexuality in recent years.

6	Norway	2009	Europe	The law replaced a 1993 statute permitting civil unions.
7	Sweden	2009	Europe	Gay and lesbian couples in Sweden previously had been allowed to register for civil unions since 1995.
8	Argentina	2010	Latin America-Caribbean	First country in Latin America to allow gay and lesbian couples to marry.
9	Iceland	2010	Europe	After the law took effect, the country's prime minister at the time, Jóhanna Sigurðardóttir, wed her longtime partner, Jónína Leósdóttir, becoming one of the first people to marry under the statute.
10	Portugal	2010	Europe	Measure passed by Parliament was approved by Portugal's Constitutional Court.
11	Denmark	2012	Europe	Same-sex marriage became legal through a separate process in Greenland, an autonomous territory of Denmark, in 2016.
12	Brazil	2013	Latin America-Caribbean	About half of Brazil's 27 jurisdictions had allowed same-sex marriage until a court ruling made it legal nationwide.
13	France	2013	Europe	Then-French President François Hollande signed the law after an unsuccessful court challenge.

14	New Zealand	2013	Asia-Pacific	First country in the Asia-Pacific region to allow gays and lesbians to wed.
15	Uruguay	2013	Latin America-Caribbean	Second Latin American country to legalize same-sex marriage, following Argentina.
16	United Kingdom	2014	Europe	Legal same-sex marriage took effect in Northern Ireland in 2020, six years after the change in England and Wales. Separate legislation was enacted in Scotland in 2014.
17	Ireland	2015	Europe	First country to legalize same-sex marriage through a popular referendum, with more than six-in-ten Irish voters (62%) in favor.
18	Luxembourg	2015	Europe	The bill was championed by the country's prime minister, Xavier Bettel, who is openly gay.
19	United States	2015	North America	Thirty-six states and the District of Columbia had legalized same-sex marriage before the U.S. Supreme Court ruled that the Constitution guarantees it throughout the country.
20	Colombia	2016	Latin America-Caribbean	Colombia's Constitutional Court legalized same-sex marriage by a 6-3 vote.
21	Australia	2017	Asia-Pacific	Voters supported legalizing same-sex marriage by a 61.6% to 38.4% margin in a non-binding nationwide referendum.

22	Finland	2017	Europe	The law, passed by Parliament in 2014, started out as a "citizens' initiative" – a public petition with nearly 167,000 signatures. It came into effect in 2017.
23	Germany	2017	Europe	Legislation passed after then-Chancellor Angela Merkel said members of her ruling Christian Democratic Union should vote their conscience even though the party formally opposed same-sex marriage.
24	Malta	2017	Europe	Parliament almost unanimously voted to legalize same-sex marriage.
25	Austria	2019	Europe	A court ruling in 2017 eventually led to the change.
26	Ecuador	2019	Latin America-Caribbean	Court ruling made Ecuador the fifth South American country to allow gays and lesbians to wed.
27	Taiwan	2019	Asia-Pacific	A court ruling prompted a change in the law that made Taiwan the first jurisdiction in Asia to permit gays and lesbians to wed.
28	Costa Rica	2020	Latin America-Caribbean	First Central American country to legalize same-sex marriage.
29	Chile	2022	Latin America-Caribbean	Sixth South American country to legalize same-sex marriage.

30	Cuba	2022	Latin America-Caribbean	Change allowing same-sex marriage was part of a broader referendum on family law that passed by a 66.9% to 33.1% vote.
31	Mexico	2022	Latin America-Caribbean	Same-sex marriage eventually became legal nationally after the Supreme Court declared state bans unconstitutional in 2015.
32	Slovenia	2022	Europe	First country in formerly communist Eastern Europe to legalize same-sex marriage.
33	Switzerland	2022	Europe	Nearly two-thirds of Swiss voters (64.1%) cast ballots in favor of legalizing same-sex marriage in a 2021 referendum.
34	Andorra	2023	Europe	Parliament in the small mountainous country between France and Spain voted to legalize same-sex marriage.

11

The Enduring Value of the Commonwealth: A Perspective from the India Region

As the Commonwealth celebrates its 75th anniversary in the year 2024, it is a time for reflection on its profound significance, particularly for the vibrant democracies of the India region. The Commonwealth transcends its historical origins; it serves as a catalyst for cooperation, institution-building, and the promotion of values essential to parliamentary democracy.

For India, a proud member of this diverse family, the Commonwealth represents more than just a coalition of nations; it embodies shared values, aspirations, and a commitment to collective progress. At its essence, the Commonwealth symbolizes unity in diversity, showcasing the power of collaboration across continents, cultures, and languages. As an Indian, I take immense pride in our nation's rich heritage and the contributions we offer to the Commonwealth's collective fabric. Our dedication to democracy, pluralism, and inclusivity resonates deeply within the Commonwealth framework, reinforcing the bonds that unite us as a community of nations.

Dr. Shanker Dayal Sharma, former president of India, aptly captured the vision of India's first Prime Minister, Jawaharlal Nehru, for the Commonwealth. Nehru believed the organization could be an instrument to support the freedom struggles of colonized nations and dismantle racism. He also envisioned the Commonwealth as a source of economic assistance for newly independent countries during their crucial initial stages. This vision was echoed in December 1948, at the Jaipur Session of the Indian National Congress. Under Nehru's guidance, a resolution was passed stating India's commitment to a free association with independent nations of the Commonwealth, working together for world peace and common welfare.

The Commonwealth's role in strengthening parliamentary democracy cannot be overstated. In an era rife with unprecedented challenges, the imperative for effective governance and democratic principles has never been more pronounced. As custodians of democracy, parliaments play a pivotal role in upholding the rule of law, safeguarding human rights, and fostering transparency and accountability.

Platforms like the Commonwealth Parliamentary Association (CPA) serve as vital conduits for this endeavor. By facilitating the exchange of ideas and best practices among parliamentarians from diverse member states, the CPA strengthens democratic institutions and fosters greater understanding and cooperation between nations.

Furthermore, the Commonwealth provides a crucial forum for dialogue and collaboration on pressing global issues, ranging from climate change to economic development to gender equality. By leveraging the collective wisdom and resources of its diverse membership, the Commonwealth amplifies the voices of member states on the global stage, advocating for inclusive solutions that benefit all.

As we commemorate this significant milestone, it is incumbent upon us to reaffirm our commitment to the ideals and principles that underpin the Commonwealth. By upholding the values of democracy, human rights, and inclusivity, we can chart a course towards a more equitable and prosperous future for all.

In conclusion, the Commonwealth holds a special place in the hearts of millions, particularly in the India region. As we reflect on its 75 years of progress and accomplishments, let us renew our resolve to collaborate and work in solidarity, paving the way for a brighter tomorrow for generations to come. Happy anniversary to the Modern Commonwealth!

●●

(Featured as a column by the author in The Parliamentarian : 2024, Issue Two – 75th anniversary edition)

Black Eagle Books

www.blackeaglebooks.org
info@blackeaglebooks.org

Black Eagle Books, an independent publisher, was founded as a nonprofit organization in April, 2019. It is our mission to connect and engage the Indian diaspora and the world at large with the best of works of world literature published on a collaborative platform, with special emphasis on foregrounding Contemporary Classics and New Writing.

www.ingramcontent.com/pod-product-compliance
Lightning Source LLC
Chambersburg PA
CBHW060616080526
44585CB00013B/854